BEYOND SOLO

BEYOND SOLO

THERE'S MORE THAN ONE WAY TO GROW YOUR BUSINESS

SARA HOWARD

First published in 2025 by Sara Howard

© Sara Howard 2025
The moral rights of the author have been asserted.

All rights reserved. Except as permitted under the *Australian Copyright Act 1968* (for example, a fair dealing for the purposes of study, research, criticism or review), no part of this book may be reproduced, stored in a retrieval system, communicated or transmitted in any form or by any means without prior written permission. No part of this book may be used or reproduced in any manner for the purpose of training artificial intelligence technologies or systems.

All inquiries should be made to the author.

A catalogue entry for this book is available from the National Library of Australia.

ISBN: 978-1-763770-50-8

Published by Whizzbang Publishing
Book production and text design by Publish Central
Cover design by Pipeline Design

The paper this book is printed on is environmentally friendly.

Disclaimer: The material in this publication is of the nature of general comment only, and does not represent professional advice. It is not intended to provide specific guidance for particular circumstances and it should not be relied on as the basis for any decision to take action or not take action on any matter which it covers. Readers should obtain professional advice where appropriate, before making any such decision. To the maximum extent permitted by law, the author and publisher disclaim all responsibility and liability to any person, arising directly or indirectly from any person taking or not taking action based on the information in this publication.

Contents

Introduction: The many roads to business growth *1*
Under pressure *1*
Exploring alternative routes *3*
At a crossroads *4*
Starting solo *5*
Flexing from solo *7*

1 The allure of freelancing *11*
The dream of freedom *12*
Why freelance? *13*
Giving freelancing a test run *20*

2 Freelancing realities *25*
Obstacles and overwhelm *26*
Getting back on track *31*

3 What does good growth look like? *37*
How to avoid a toxic growth spiral *38*
Good reasons to grow *43*
Making growth work for you *46*
Five ways to get growth right *48*
How to take your value seriously *50*
What happens if your growth plan stalls? *53*
What happens if your growth plan gets turbocharged? *54*

4 The Five Ps powering good growth 59
The foundation for every business growth model 60
Pack your Five Ps for your growth journey 76

5 Beyond solo to culture-led growth: build your ideal business 81
Build the business you'd drop everything to work for 82
What *is* culture? 83
The benefits of a small but mighty culture 83
Defining your culture 85
Making sure your culture sticks as you grow 94

6 Beyond solo to hybrid: outsourcing 97
Start here if you're not ready to hire 98
You can't do it all 99
Right people, right seats 101
To outsource or not to outsource? 107

7 Beyond solo to small business: the traditional growth model 113
Now that you're your own boss, are you ready to be the boss? 114
The in-house staff advantage 118
The hidden risks of taking on staff 120
Who you need on board 122
What do you offer as an employer? 123
Hiring well 125
Where will you find this person? 128
How much do you need to pay people? 129
Who don't you need to hire? 130
Becoming the best boss you can 131
How to stretch your capacity and stay in control 135
Setting yourself up for success 139

Time-saving systems and processes *145*
Get into a workflow rhythm *148*
Propositions and pipeline *148*
Keep following up *156*

8 Beyond solo to collective: A-Team collaboration *161*

Tapping into the expertise of likeminded freelancers *162*
The different collective models *163*
Aligning incentives *174*
Scaling a collective *175*

9 Beyond solo to set-and-forget income: subscriptions and products *179*

Want to make money while you sleep? Here's what that takes *180*
Where do product ideas come from? *181*
Not all products are revenue-makers *184*
Turning DIY tools into a win–win *185*
Creating a product ecosystem *188*
The Five Ps and productising your business *197*
Are products really worth the effort? *199*

10 The good growth reality check *203*

Sustaining your mojo when the going gets tough *204*
Up isn't the only way *205*
Take control where you can *207*

11 Beyond solo to exit strategy *217*

Getting the most from your business when it's time to move on *218*
Stop, succession or sell *219*
Exploring all your exit options *234*

12 The next step 241
Ready to make good growth happen for you? 242
Avoiding a growth hangover 242
How do you know which path to take? 243
Stepping out of your comfort zone 244
Start your engine 246
You are here 247

Gratitude 249

Acknowledgements 251

Introduction
The many roads to business growth

On the surface, everything looked great. My business, a copywriting agency called Writers, was humming along, growing steadily every year. We had a solid client list of high-calibre companies and regular recurring work. We consistently received positive feedback and referrals, and our project pipeline was always full. Clients asked if they could prepay us to lock in their budget. My team said they felt supported and had opportunities to learn.

For someone who spent all day playing with words, I was also earning decent money.

So, why did I often feel trapped?

Under pressure

Why did my heart start racing in a panicky way every time another brief or meeting request landed in my inbox? I should be happy about the new work, right?

How had I lost control over where and how I spent my time? Why was I constantly working overtime just to keep my head above water?

What could I do differently to overcome the tension and burden my body was expressing through clenched jaw and aching shoulders? There were times I knew I'd lost the joy in the work. To be frank, I'd started resenting it.

We were growing, but a nagging voice in my brain thought, *maybe not as much as we should be given how much pressure I feel.*

That pressure was partly the crushing weight of responsibility. This was my company, and people were counting on me to make it work – not just so they could get paid every month but because they felt part of something.

When friends asked me how it was going, I'd reply 'busy', and they'd tell me that was a good problem to have. Yet it didn't always feel good – for my mental health, my relationships or my sleep.

That's when I began wondering about all the paths I didn't take and how I had ended up on a one-way street to 'busy'.

Strategy is not just a series of decisions about what to do. It's also a conscious choice about what *not* to do.

Over a decade earlier, I'd made a conscious choice to hire my first employee. That started my journey along the traditional small creative agency route. But if there had been a signpost at the time signalling the other roads I could take, perhaps my journey would have been smoother. Or perhaps I would have had fewer moments of self-doubt along the way.

That's what this book is about. It's your signposted crossroad. As a freelancer or independent consultant, you will get to a certain point where you might decide you want more. You want to grow. Or perhaps you want less. And you need to know what your options are.

This is the book I needed all those years ago.

Exploring alternative routes

This book might help you course-correct if you feel you're on the wrong road or want to change vehicles. It doesn't have to mean heading off in a completely new direction. You don't need to take the first freeway exit or a meandering back road. You can just slow down and enjoy the view.

Or bring different people along for the ride.

Alternative routes might include outsourcing certain tasks to free up your time instead of managing them in-house. They could also mean creating a collective, which would give you the chance to work with other experts without the salary overhead, or building a passive income stream from products, courses or communities.

Ultimately, your destination is also up to you. You need to know where *your* exit is. We'll go through those choices too, so you can (if you want) plan the best route.

First, I want to reassure you that I no longer feel trapped. And I certainly don't have any regrets. In the process of researching this book, I spoke with agency owners and other bigger-business founders about what they've learned along the way. I checked in with clients too – because it's no use creating a business model if it doesn't work for your customers. And I learned so much by talking with freelancers and consultants – people like you – who have pursued different models for growth.

In many cases, they found a better way that works for them.

Others, not so much. Over coffee with one former client, he remarked how my 'elegant, smooth, mature business arc' contrasts with his 'decade of lunacy'.

While I feel anything but mature, elegant or smooth – even on a good day – his decade of lunacy included a triple heart bypass and being swindled by a Mexican event organiser.

It's certainly a different journey to mine. And yours will be different too.

At a crossroads

This book is for you if:

- you're just embarking on your freelance journey, and you want a clearer roadmap
- you're too busy with freelance work to breathe, let alone bring someone on to help
- you're finding this freelance lark a bit lonely, or you need to get out of a rut
- you have an idea for a passive income stream or set-and-forget product, but you're not sure it's worth pursuing
- you know you need some financial systems and processes, and you're looking for a shortcut
- you'd like to hire staff but you're nervous about being the boss
- you'd like to build a business that will have saleable value one day
- you'd like to run a business that could outlast you, or leave a legacy.

It's also for anyone who wants to know all their options before starting on their freelance journey.

I hope you'll feel it's for you.

Please write, draw, and experiment throughout the book – this is your journey! Throughout the book, there are spaces for you to pause, reflect on what works for you and make some notes. If you need more space, grab a notebook.

Starting solo

Before we begin, let's wind back the clock. Close your eyes, and visualise the moment you made the decision to set out on your own.

It might be quite recent, or it might be many years ago. Maybe you're still weighing up the pros and cons, and you're hoping this book will give you that final shot of confidence. No matter what stage you're at, I want you to picture that pivotal moment when you decided to quit the day job and start up on your own.

Keep that moment front and centre as you read this book and consider all the options you now have. Even as everything else in your life evolves, your original motivation doesn't change – because your desire to build something of your own, or feel in control of your day, or keep stretching yourself, is still a constant.

For me, it took some wise advice to work out how I could meet my need for income with a sense of purpose. Picture this: I'm sitting at a dining table crammed into my unrenovated kitchen. My toddler is crawling across the linoleum floor, his brother is building Lego in the corner. My friend Renee is nursing a cup of tea, and in my sleep-deprived brain fog I'm hoping she'll help me work out what to do next in my stop–start post-parenthood career.

I'd spent three years running a baby t-shirt business from the spare room, in the precious few childcare hours available. One of that growing cohort of 'mumpreneurs' – a demeaning label that made the very real stress of juggling childcare and playdates with deadlines and cashflow seem cute.

I'd enjoyed the creativity of my micro business, but not the boxes of stock that had taken over our spare room, or the long days hauling that stock around markets and babywear retailers. Or the fact it barely covered costs – we needed to put a bigger dent in the mortgage.

But I had an unexpected opportunity. My husband was being transferred to England for one year, and our expenses would be covered. One of the retailers who stocked my baby t-shirts was taking the business (and all those boxes of stock) off my hands.

Once I'd worked out the net gain from that sale, I could just about afford to ... buy a new laptop.

But I also had something far more valuable: time.

I told Renee my modest career criteria: flexible around the kids, with enough pay to at least cover the cost of daycare.

She suggested I study copywriting. It was still the early days of online content, and she knew I'd always wanted to be a writer. But I had no idea what copywriters did. I had a horrible feeling it might be linked to trademarks and IP law, which sounded dull.

Once I discovered copywriting involved creativity, curiosity and putting words down on paper, I was hooked. I found an online course I could complete during our year in England. My tutor on that course also ran a copywriting agency in Bristol, Writers Ltd. He and his partners asked to meet with me when I finished the course, and in one of those life-changing moments of serendipity, I agreed to set up the Sydney office of Writers Australia.

I will be forever grateful to them for taking a chance on me, because they gave me advice on every word I wrote in my first professional projects.

However, running my own business was actually never part of my plan. Through my 20s, I pursued my dream career in retail buying, working in London and then the US. I learned the hard way that working for a corporate did not equal financial security when I lost my job and quickly had to move home to Sydney – pregnant and unemployed at 30.

Under these circumstances, the only thing I thought I could do to feel in control, to have choice over the structure of my days and the decisions that affected me financially, was to work for myself.

Flexing from solo

It didn't take me long to work out working from home didn't work for me. I needed to get away from the piles of laundry and Lego every day. I also wanted to close the door on work at the end of the day and focus on my family. So I found an office – a small room above a local bookstore – within walking distance of my home and the kids' school.

I was also lonely. I longed for someone to bounce ideas around with. Wearing all the hats in my business wasn't as much fun as I'd imagined. There were most definitely a lot of tasks someone else could do better.

And finally, I really wanted to take a holiday. I missed travelling, and I wanted to see the world through my kids' eyes. But I didn't want my fledgling business to grind to a halt while I took three weeks off.

So I decided to grow. Slowly, carefully. Without putting my house on the line, and while still paying myself a decent salary and superannuation.

I learned how to do that by talking to lots of smart people, because that was my job.

> Every time I researched an article about business strategy, or workplace culture, or leadership, or cashflow, or sales frameworks, I'd think *maybe I can do that too.*

And those experiments and ideas helped my business keep growing.

I also made a lot of mistakes along the way. I chased growth for the wrong reasons. I brought in people who weren't the right fit for what we needed at that moment.

I'll share all those highs and lows with you in this book. The book I wished I'd had when I first started.

Ready? Let's go.

Before we begin – some important fine print:

I am absolutely not an accountant or tax professional and am not qualified to give you any financial advice. All the ideas, frameworks and models in this book are based on my own experience and that of others, and they are just a starting point for you to consider and discuss with your own trusted advisers. There may also be aspects that simply don't apply where you operate, or for your type of business or services.

Throughout this book, you'll read firsthand accounts from dozens of business owners and solo operators about the things that have (and haven't) worked for them on their own journey. These insights represent a moment in time, and their situation and business structure may have changed since then. Without their input, this book wouldn't have anywhere near as much wisdom or value, and I appreciate their generosity and honesty in sharing their stories with us. I continue to learn so much from everyone I speak with.

More choice, more control, more flexibility, and (maybe) more money. That's the liberating potential of freelancing.

1: The allure of freelancing

The dream of freedom

The very word 'freelance' implies freedom. And that's why so many people choose to take the plunge – they want to feel more in control of where, when and how they work.

Does that sound like you?

In the United States, freelancing is a mainstream phenomenon. Over 21 million Americans are now freelancing full-time – around a third of the 60 million Americans who are independent workers. The fastest growing segment here is the 'side hustler', supplementing other paid work with freelance gigs.[1]

It's a little less prevalent in the United Kingdom and Australia. According to ABS data, over one million Australians work as independent contractors[2] and a further 800,000 run sole-trader businesses.[3] That means around 14% of Australia's working population are solo professionals for hire.

The proportion is similar in the UK, with around 1.9 million freelancers.[4] More than half have been freelancing for 10 or more years, so they're well-established independent operators.

Apart from the many personal motivations to freelance, which we'll explore in this chapter, independent professionals have experienced growing demand for their skills.

Post-COVID, companies were scrambling to find talented people who could get all the work done. A pause on hiring budgets made freelancers even more attractive.

---

1 State of Independence in America, MBO Partners 2022.
2 ABS data as at August 2022: 1.1 million independent contractors. Total employment Sept. 2023 14,115,100.
3 ABS data as at 30 June 2023: 784,744 sole proprietors; 2,589,873 actively trading businesses.
4 *The Self-Employed Landscape Report 2022*, IPSE.

Freelance platform Fiverr found 78% of US companies planned to rely on freelancers rather than add staff.[5]

With most companies having already adapted to working remotely, collaborating with freelancers is as easy as working with a hybrid in-house team. It also gives companies access to specialised skills for short-term projects.

For better or worse, generative AI is now shifting demand for freelance skills. Analysis of Upwork data from 2022 to 2024 – that period when AI suddenly emerged as an everyday tool for just about every type of knowledge work – indicated demand for some job categories – including video editing, web design and development – actually grew. How that will continue to evolve remains to be seen.[6]

Why freelance?

The number-one motivation to go freelance is that you get to be in charge of when you choose to work – which days and what time of day. That's according to HR platform Remote's survey of 3000 business owners, freelancers and employees in the US and UK.[7]

It's interesting to see how their expectations of freelancing measure up to reality. Over half those freelancers admitted being your own boss is easier than they expected.

A significant proportion also valued freelancing as a way to build their confidence. This is interesting, because it suggests as we step up, take on more responsibilities, run our own show and

---

[5] Fiverr survey conducted in partnership with Censuswide, August 2022.
[6] 'The Jobs Being Replaced by AI: An analysis of 5M freelancing jobs', Upwork data analysis, February 2024.
[7] 'Remote's Global Freelancer Report: The state of play in 2023'.

say yes to projects that stretch us, we are developing confidence in our skills.

And because we are our own boss, we still feel in control when we say yes to things that challenge us.

Feeling in control of our hours, workload and future is a compelling motivator. After all, autonomy increases your sense of wellbeing and self-esteem – it's a fundamental human need.

When I lost my corporate job at 29, I realised the stability of a full-time job is an illusion.

> You cannot take anything for granted in a business you have no control over.

Flexing around family

UK data shows the number of freelance working mothers increased by 79% in the 12 years to 2020[8] – and they are more likely to work in higher skilled professional and technical freelance roles. For many working parents, freelancing has the allure of true flexibility – no one will question your need to balance the school run with your meeting schedule. You can work around Easter hat parades or school trips and be present in your kid's life when it matters to them.

I spoke with many freelancers while researching this book. A significant number – both men and women – told me having children was either a catalyst for jumping ship into freelancing or for taking their freelancing more seriously.

---

[8] IPSE data: 'Women in Self-Employment: Understanding the female self-employed community'.

Jo Marshall, the UK-based founder of All Things Words, was a director in a small copywriting agency when she was ready to start her family. She realised she would need more flexibility and control at that point – not only over her time, but also over the type of work she did.

'As a freelancer, when my kids were little I was able to scale my work right back to two days a week – and just about make that work financially. I'm really grateful my business gave me that flexibility,' she says.

> 'I wanted to be able to play to my strengths in that time, and have **more choice over the work I wanted to do**.'
>
> Jo Marshall

Amy Ragland is a freelance financial services writer based in the US. She says she missed contributing financially to her family when her children were very young, and sought an identity outside mothering.

'Freelancing helped me feel like I was doing something that was all mine. I don't think we talk enough about the importance of keeping something that's just for *you*, that isn't tied into your identity as a wife, mother or daughter,' she says.

'Freelancing also gave me the opportunity to find balance between work and family – my husband and I decided one of us needed flexibility in our days (around school hours or if someone was sick), and I was in a better position professionally to be able to make that happen.'

Ed Gandia, a US-based coach, says once his first son was born, he took a hard look at his corporate sales role and realised weekly travel would be inevitable.

'I know how I'm wired; I'm very driven, and I was afraid that lifestyle wasn't going to end well for me or my family,' he says. 'In sales, the better you do, the more is expected of you – you can't take a step back. It's easy to get caught up in that.'

For Ed, freelancing gave him control over where and how he spent his time while his kids were little. Now he focuses on helping other people build that lifestyle with a successful business coaching other freelancers.

Australian journalist Carolyn Tate says being a single mum added an extra layer of pressure to make freelancing work: 'I was going through a divorce, and my son had a lot of needs. I couldn't work full time. So, I decided I had to make freelance work for me.' Eight years on, it's no longer what Carolyn describes as a 'white-knuckle ride'. She is consistently busy and is looking at ways to grow her business, Stellar Content.

As all these freelancers admit, the feast-or-famine reality of freelancing while supporting a family is challenging. It's also worth noting that it's not always necessary to give up a job you love to have some degree of flexibility, with a hybrid work-from-home culture increasingly the norm for knowledge workers.

Ultimate control

For some freelancers, the desire for control is also about achieving that elusive goal of work/life balance. Again, the reality of working from home – whether on your own terms or someone else's – is that it's more of a work/life blend. While the commute is infinitely shorter, it takes discipline to close the door on work at the end of the day.

Control can also mean greater choice over clients and projects, as Jo Marshall discovered when she focused fully on a sector she cared deeply about.

'As I got older, it became increasingly important to me to do work I really believe in, and I do genuinely believe in what universities are doing, and all the knowledge and opportunities that are being created,' she says. 'So a few years ago, I went all in on just writing for higher education clients.'

Like Jo, you might want to pursue an area that gives you purpose – such as working with not-for-profits or combining creativity with strategy.

Or you may want more variety – you might be bored with the same subject matter every day, or be seeking the chance to diversify your income stream. This also helps you avoid being tied to one industry, which can be risky if it's hit especially hard by a market downturn.

For those still unencumbered by parenting responsibilities, control can also mean the ability to combine travel with work. A staggering 16.9 million Americans describe themselves as digital nomads,[9] using technology to work from anywhere in the world. Several countries – including Indonesia and Portugal – now offer digital nomad visas to enable this growing class of temporary migrants.

For some, the shift to freelancing is due to factors beyond their control. They may be unable to work in their previous role due to illness or disability, and freelancing from home allows them to manage their condition and put their skills to work. They may have unexpected caring responsibilities for an ageing

---

9   'State of Independence in America', MBO Partners 2022.

parent or sick partner. Or a redundancy might force their hand – and provide a final catalyst for a long-held desire to be their own boss.

Freelance writer Oyelola Oyetunji was close to burnout with a major global consultancy firm when she started feeling overwhelming fatigue and joint pain. She stepped away from her job and picked up some work writing tenders for her previous manager, who was now running a fintech. By the time those tenders won a major contract, she'd been diagnosed with Lupus – a debilitating autoimmune disease.

While she worked through lifestyle changes to manage her condition, Oyelola kept writing. And she realised she not only loved writing more than consulting, but she was also really good at it.

'I'd heard about the concept of copywriting before, but I thought it was about legal copyright,' she laughs. 'The more I researched it, the more I thought this is what I want to do. And when I turned the corner with Lupus in 2020, I decided to start a freelance writing business.'

Oyelola's business, Phrased with Purpose, focuses on smaller businesses with a positive impact: 'I found that when I started writing for solopreneurs interested in the greater good, I started to come alive.'

Ultimate control can also be good for your bank balance. As freelance thought leadership writer Tom Mangan shared on LinkedIn, 'My biggest surprise was saying "this is how much money I want", and people would pay it. This is not part of the model of employment: a boss puts you on the payroll and marks up the value of your labour … Self-employment lets me keep a bunch of that markup – and the only insufferable boss I have to put up with is me.'[10]

Higher-calibre exposure

Many fractional consultants and experienced freelancers enjoy the challenges of stepping into high-stakes projects with a defined timeframe and outcome. They're respected for the expertise they bring and often work with senior leaders they'd rarely connect with as an employee in a siloed corporate.

My own projects have taken me into boardrooms, multinational strategy sessions and MBA schools. I've learned to quickly build trust with CEOs on Zoom calls and get deep inside complex business structures. Most of all, I've discovered the joy of getting hands-on with a project without having to kowtow to office politics or twiddle my thumbs in pointless internal meetings.

Pete Cohen, an Australia-based innovation coach and consultant, has pivoted between in-house roles and freelancing throughout his technology career. He says variety is a big part of why he keeps going back to freelancing. Also, the working relationships are better.

'I think there's something in the timebound nature of the work. We know it's not forever. We're here to explore a specific problem and make some progress in that. And that means I meet people at a particular level, rather than as an employee subordinate.'

Pete is currently experimenting with cooperative structures for freelancers. He says independent knowledge workers still need

---

10 https://www.linkedin.com/posts/edgandia_selfemployment-worklifebalance-burnoutawareness-activity-7171489822828548096-hAEh.

community to be able to bounce ideas and collaborate with a tribe.

We'll take a closer look at cooperatives and collectives in chapter 8.

Giving freelancing a test run

You don't have to give up your day job straightaway.

Many people test the freelancing waters with a side hustle outside their nine-to-five job, or blend part-time work with consulting.

Sarah Spence spent several years juggling a part-time role in a local creative agency with 10 to 15 hours of freelance retainer work a week. 'My biggest worry was that I wouldn't be able to replace my salary if I left my job, but it got to the point where I was turning down projects I'd much rather do,' she says.

In Sarah's first year as a freelancer, she earned twice her previous salary. We'll explore how she grew her agency by blending an in-house team with a pool of subcontractors later in this book.

Successful freelancers start from a strong base: they have enough confidence in their own abilities to find a client willing to pay what they're worth. They know how to price for the value they bring. They are willing to say yes to things that will stretch them – and say no to things that don't smell right.

Most consultants find saying yes easy, because it's in our nature to help. Also, there's an unspoken fear that if we say no, we'll never work again.

Saying yes to things that stretch you takes a bit more courage. When I first started, everything was outside my comfort zone. I absolutely faked it in many early meetings. I still remember the heart palpitations in my first meeting with a creative agency director to discuss a commercial property campaign.

'Can you write an IM?' she asked.

'Sure, no problem,' I said.

And then googled *what is an IM* on the bus home.[11]

Saying no can be really challenging, especially if you're a natural people-pleaser.

But if you have started freelancing with freedom as your goal, you cannot say yes to everything.

You will end up trading all the security of a salaried job for a different kind of cage, trapped in projects you don't love with people you don't like.

I have learned this lesson the hard way. The projects that negatively impacted my sleep, mood or relationships were absolutely the ones I should have turned down. I remember questioning the objective of a particularly obtuse campaign brief with another creative director. 'To win me an award,' he replied.

That's not why I write. I want to help clients make an impact with their ideas or inspire action or positive change. I walked away from that job as quickly as I could.

---

11 Turns out it's an 'information memorandum', which is a very dull name for a commercial property brochure.

Whether you're just starting out on your freelancing journey or have many years under your belt, saying no to clients like that guy is still hard when your project pipeline is unpredictable. Or if your inner critic has you convinced you'll never get work again.

That's just one of the many realities of running your own show, which we'll explore in chapter 2.

LET'S GROW

Take a moment to reflect on where you are right now in your freelancing journey.

1. Why did you decide to freelance, in just one word?

   ....

2. Is that a reality in this moment?

   ....

   ....

   ....

   ....

   ....

   ....

   ....

3. What's one thing you're missing right now?

   ....

   ....

   ....

   ....

   ....

   ....

   ....

'Left unchecked, **freelancing can turn into a 60-hour-per-week job**, with no flexibility, vacations or creative freedom.'

Ed Gandia

2: Freelancing realities

Obstacles and overwhelm

Given the choice, why *wouldn't* you trade working for a rigid boss for feeling in control of where, when and how you work?

Unfortunately, that trade-off doesn't always work out in your favour.

'Freelancing can also become a nightmare,' says Ed Gandia. 'Many freelancers feel under the gun to meet deadlines and take meetings. Their weeks are stressful and filled with work they dislike.'

How does this happen?

The problem is twofold: time and money.

If you're under pressure to make the mortgage or rent, you'll do whatever it takes to get the work in.

But there's just not enough time to do it all. Suddenly, you're faced with a tsunami of projects surging towards your to-do list. Your heart starts racing. You can't think clearly. Even if it's work you find interesting, it doesn't bring you joy. Worse, it takes you away from family and friends, and you start to resent it.

Oh yes, I've been there.

Then there's the guilt. You're packing for a family holiday, having spent the last week working until midnight to get ahead of the deadlines, and your kid begs you to leave your laptop at home so you can play with them in the pool.

But how can you respond to clients if you do that?

And then suddenly, the work dries up. Project schedules get pushed back. Your biggest client has been made redundant. There's been a budget cut. Or your favourite small business client is now using AI to do a lot of what you used to charge them for.

Or maybe it's just a slow week.

Immediately, you're convinced you'll never get another freelance job again. Going back to the day job suddenly feels alluring.

Many freelancers get stuck in this feast-or-famine cycle.

If spiralling downwards in that cycle sounds familiar, you'll find some tips on how to break that pattern in the next few chapters. We'll also explore different ways to bring other people on board, so you can flex your capacity and avoid the overwhelm.

One can be the loneliest number

Employment can provide a sense of belonging and social connection that freelancing cannot replace. Over 50% of Australian freelancers surveyed feared a lack of connection to a company's internal culture would leave them feeling like outsiders.[12]

Amy Ragland says the loneliness of freelancing took her by surprise.

'I'm a big introvert and don't mind working on my own,' she admits. 'But it's hard to "talk shop" with people in my life because they just don't get it.'

She also says freelancing can feel like working in a vacuum because she is removed from the final impact of her work and often gets no feedback. While getting more work from the same

---

12 *Suicide Prevention Australia, Submission 181*, cited in Select Committee on Job Security report, Feb. 2022.

client is always a positive sign, she knows she can't grow if she doesn't know what to fix.

That feeling of isolation can be a powerful motivator to think about growing your business beyond you.

Perhaps you've realised all the business admin – sending quotes, chasing invoices, dealing with the tax office, creating LinkedIn post carousels and client emails – is not your strength. It would be nice to have someone to share the load.

Building an agency model not only gave me the ability to offload some of those tasks and get more work done. It also helped me develop as a writer. From day one, we implemented a robust peer review process. By editing each other's work, we are always learning where we can improve, and can share different approaches to any given brief.

Risky business

There are sometimes hidden risks in freelancing, especially when you're just starting out.

> A project setback can put a dent in your confidence and your bank balance.

Web designer Jordanne Collins learned the insidious impact of scope creep the hard way on her first WordPress website design.

'I was subcontracting to a studio, and it didn't have a formal scope of works agreement with the client. I was paid one project fee – and six months of revisions later, I was losing money on the job,' she admits.

Despite this, she fell in love with web design on that job. She acknowledges she learned some valuable skills – not just in WordPress, but in setting up systems and being firm with expectations and requirements.

'Now I have processes for everything. When I onboard clients, I have a timeline with specific content and feedback deadlines. My contracts have clauses tied to those, and if they're not met there are delay fees.'

So far, she's yet to apply those delay fees. But it means clients take her processes more seriously.

The momentum of Oyelola Oyetunji's freelance writing business took a knock when she lost three retainer clients at once.

'Growth felt effortless in my second year, with lots of clients going online and needing regular content. And then, three cut their budgets. All at once,' she told me.

That was when Oyelola realised she had to be more proactive with marketing: 'It took me a while to find my voice online. I decided to play to my strengths and go back to more in-person networking, building and nurturing relationships. That changed everything.'

It takes resilience to bounce back from setbacks like these. It also takes grace to acknowledge the lessons they deal you, and make changes accordingly.

The insidious toll of instability

The biggest challenge freelancers share is managing an irregular income.[13] Cashflow can have seasonal dips over summer and

---

13 'Remote's Global Freelancer Report: The state of play in 2023'.

Christmas – but the mortgage still needs to be paid. If you can even get that home loan approved.

Financial uncertainty makes it difficult to plan for the future.

> Knowledge work is notoriously stop-start. It's everything-is-at-stake urgent, and then it's suddenly on hold until after Christmas.

Project pivots are a minor frustration for the client, but it's an income black hole for the freelancer who said no to three other jobs thinking this stalled project would keep them busy for the next six weeks.

Managing expectations with clients can be tough. How can you push back on unrealistic budgets or deadlines when you also want to foster a good relationship so they trust your work?

There are also costs you may not have budgeted for – all those software subscriptions, insurance premiums, and web hosting fees can add up.

As a result, you may be more in control of your hours but you're likely to work harder and longer. US and UK freelancers tend to work more unpaid overtime than employees, at an average of 9.7 hours per week compared to 7.4 for employees.[14]

Professor Cary Cooper, professor of organisational psychology and health at MBS Manchester University, has described the irregular hours, isolation and financial pressure of freelancing as a stress generator. Along with being unable to switch off, these factors can also lead to depression and anxiety.[15]

---

14 Ibid.
15 'I felt "vulnerable": Freelancers on the stress of self-employment', *The Guardian*, December 2016.

And this, in turn, can create more financial pressure. There's no paid sick leave when you're a freelancer.

No way out?

You started freelancing for control. But at a certain point, you might be so busy managing the day-to-day demands of pitching for work, getting that work done, chasing approvals, sending invoices, answering emails, setting up new business meetings, posting on socials, chasing payments ... there's no time to think beyond the next eight hours, let alone plan for the longer term.

That might prompt you to wonder how you climb off the hamster wheel. Do you just turn off your laptop one day? Could you ever sell your business if it depends on you? We'll explore the answer to these questions in chapter 11.

Getting back on track

One way to deal with the natural ebbs and flows of freelance income is to be disciplined in how you structure your finances. As a former finance professional, Amy Ragland has grounded her business in a simple financial management system. Every project fee goes into her business bank account, and then she allocates:

- 35% to business savings for taxes and future expenses
- 10% to her retirement account
- 5% for business expenses
- 50% to her personal account as earned income.

If you start thinking of your personal income as 50% of the total fees you earn, how might that change your approach to rates?

Ed Gandia suggests most freelancers could do three things more effectively before they start worrying about growth strategies:

- **Raise your fees:** either by increasing your rates or focusing on higher value work.
- **Be more efficient:** get serious about your productivity and how you structure your days.
- **Take on more recurring work:** for more predictable cashflow and even more efficiency.

'You need at least two out of those three, and ideally all three,' he says. 'If you do that, you're addressing the underlying problems. Scaling your business isn't going to fix the existing issues, it just magnifies them.'

We'll dig deeper into how you do each of these things in the next few chapters. So even if you want to stay as a company of one, keep reading.

Ed admits he's hit roadblocks of his own over the years. One-on-one coaching is impossible to scale as it has a time-based ceiling. So, he shifted to group coaching – and that achieved two things, one of which he did not anticipate.

'Obviously, it meant I could take on more people at the same time. But there's an added collaboration benefit. Most people I work with prefer this model because they learn much more from the group conversations. We ended up creating a community, and it has opened up more possibilities for me.'

Those possibilities include workshops and courses that are almost entirely passive income. And it wouldn't have happened unless Ed found a way to tackle a very common challenge that most successful freelancers face: the need to work excessive hours to keep up with demand.

Freelancers are finding ways to manage the unexpected downsides of being solo. But it can be hard to find the right balance when you're on your own. And any potential business growth is constrained by time – you can only earn so much in the hours you have each day.

So what are your options? Let's start by defining what growth might look like for you. Because not all growth is good, as we'll explore in the next chapter.

LET'S GROW

Before you move on, be honest with yourself about your freelance business as it currently stands.

1. Which of these challenges resonates most with you? Tick as many as you like.

    - ☐ Too much work, and not enough time.
    - ☐ Not enough work, which means financial stress.
    - ☐ Unpredictable work and income.
    - ☐ The unexpected costs of running a business.
    - ☐ Anxiety about unknown risks.
    - ☐ Client expectations beyond my capabilities.
    - ☐ Loneliness.
    - ☐ Self-doubt.
    - ☐ Something else ....

2. If you could change one thing about how you work, what would it be?

NOTES

Bigger is not always better. But what does 'better' mean for you anyway?

3: What does good growth look like?

How to avoid a toxic growth spiral

We think of growth as a byproduct of success, and that it means 'more'. More income. More work. More people. More opportunities you wouldn't have had otherwise.

Growth can also mean 'less': less pressure on you to be responsible for everything. That sounds good, right?

Not always.

We typically think of business growth as numbers on an upward trajectory – revenue, staff and (hopefully) profit. Western work culture glorifies the entrepreneurial hustle. Working every hour you can, taking on responsibility for more people, saying yes to every open door.

Gordon Gecko's commentary on greed in the movie *Wall Street* rang hollow, even in the 1980s. The thing is, we all know who greed *isn't* working for: the small operators.

It might be the same with growth.

What goes on beneath the surface of small business growth may be far from good. It might not be good for your sleep or mental health. It may not even be profitable.

Growth is not unlimited because it always comes at a cost. It takes time, money, resources and compromise.

I see good growth as more than numbers moving upwards. It's a mindset: being intentional about how you grow, rather than growing for the sake of growing. More flexible than a 10-year business strategy with Big Hairy Audacious Goals and stretch targets. And the opposite of growth for ego – which is to prove your success, calculate your value or have something to brag about at parties.

Regenerative models for growth

Good growth is sustainable, in that it sustains every aspect of your life for as long as you need it to. But it can also be sustainable in other meaningful ways. Because there is something else the 'greed/growth is good' mantra doesn't work for, and that's the planet.

Watching a documentary about regenerative farming practices, I was struck by the idea of creating the right environment for growth – in this case, the soil – and then letting nature do the work. Without chemical intervention but with careful and conscious management.

Regenerative business models have a very precise purpose: restoring and regenerating natural resources and social systems. Making things better rather than merely reducing harm. 'Regenerative business model' is also a term that has been greenwashed into many business strategies. That's not what I'm suggesting here. But it might be helpful to think of growth within the regenerative mindset.

> Think qualitative growth, rather than quantitative. Making things better, not just bigger.

Qualitative metrics might include skills and knowledge growth, community building, or the ability to solve more complex problems.

Growth targets vs growth boundaries

For me, good growth starts with defining what is enough – and that's quantitative and qualitative.

What does *enough* mean to you? Your answer to that question might be very different to your coworking neighbour.
And that's okay.

'Everyone's growth will be different,' says Amy Ragland. For Amy, work needs to fit with her stage of life – and when her daughters head off to college, her business might look different again. She says:

> 'Too many freelancers get stuck in the comparison game. My life doesn't look like anyone else's – and my freelance business won't either.'

Amy runs a solo freelance practice, but being solo doesn't stop her from growing. She is intentional about increasing her income by setting three income targets at the beginning of every year: 'My standard goal is usually 8% to 10% above the prior year. I've hit it every year but one.'

Her stretch goals add another 10% to that target, which she says is challenging but doable. And her challenging goal adds another 10% over that. She won't be devastated if she doesn't reach it – but she knows she won't maintain her disciplined approach if she doesn't push herself that bit further.

Amy is also clear that growth is not solely about financial targets. It's also about professional and personal growth. That also means balancing the desire to stretch herself with acknowledging she can't be everything to everyone. She says: 'If I'm doing the same thing year after year, I'm not growing professionally. I also want to work on projects that are meaningful and helpful to people.'

I'm really impressed by Amy's discipline in hitting these growth targets year on year. To grow 10% every year on your own is hard: you can only do so much by increasing your rates. At a certain point, you either have to take on much higher value work, or work more hours. Or perhaps get technology to automate a big chunk of what you do.

For Amy, *enough* is about stretching herself just the right amount.

Your *enough* might be less elastic. Like Brooke Hill, who was made redundant from her corporate role when she had a three-week-old baby. She defined her *enough* as being able to work no more than 10 contracted hours a week.

'Within months, I had to think about how I'd manage the workload. For me, that meant subcontracting,' she says. A content agency evolved from that conscious choice – and eight years later, Brooke still works those reduced hours at Wonderthink.

'Good business growth means growing sustainably while growing profit. For me, it means not burning out. It means spending as much time with my family or on my work as I choose. And it means loving what I do,' she says.

There's a common thread to both Brooke's and Amy's approach, and it involves setting boundaries. Knowing when to say no is powerful. We'll explore that more in chapter 5.

The hidden cost of more

There's a certain amount of ego attached to growing a small business – it signals success to friends, family, society and future clients. But that's not *why* you grow.

It took me a very long time to realise not all growth is good. For too long, I thought the only way to grow was to take on *more*.

More work, more staff, more responsibilities, more meetings, more deadlines, more pressure.

Yes, that meant my income was more too. But there was a cost, and it was sometimes my happiness. It was the time I didn't spend with my kids during the school holidays. All the other things I had to say no to.

I don't regret the choices I made on that journey, as they taught me growth isn't the only measure of success.

I also learned how far I could comfortably stretch my *enough* elastic band. As my kids grew, we made conscious choices to travel as a family and invest in their education. But we didn't aspire to a bigger house or another car.

Enough meant my business just had to sustain those choices.

Enough doesn't need to be pegged to a top salary bracket. These days, it's not so much about money as time and flexibility for me. I've come full circle in my independent professional career, back to the very first reasons I started.

Your choices will be different. And that's okay.

Simon Bedard has helped hundreds of companies through his consultancy Exit Advisory in Australia. A number of his buy, sell and succession plan clients are dealing with growth roadblocks.

'Growth for the sake of growth is usually unhealthy,' he tells me. 'One client recently told me his business was by all measures successful, but he was miserable. He was spending all his time dealing with people problems.'

To make things worse, this client wasn't generating much income for himself. Simon helped him pull back his business to the things he enjoyed doing.

'Once you start scaling back, you can make better decisions about the types of clients you want to work with,' he observes.

Defining what is enough can make your boundaries much easier to enforce. In his book *Company of One*, Paul Jarvis describes a 'focus on getting better, rather than bigger'. He believes staying small can be an end goal, and it can also be a smart long-term strategy.

'All business is a choice about the life we want outside of it,' he writes.[16]

What could be more liberating than that?

Good reasons to grow

Ed Gandia makes his living coaching other freelancers to grow – and he says around 15% of his clients want to scale their business beyond themselves.

Ed says: 'My first question is always, "why?" We need to take money out of the equation, because there's a limit to what growth can give you. Then I ask, "what do you want to do more of in your business?"'

He explains:

> 'As you grow, you'll have to manage more people, more processes, more workflows. Is that what you really want?'

As a business content writer, I've interviewed hundreds of business owners and leaders about strategy and growth.

---

16 *Company of One*, Paul Jarvis, Mariner Books 2019.

I'd describe one longstanding client, a major bank, as my mini-MBA – almost every good strategy idea I've had for my own business has come from the conversations they pay me to have.

In one example, a financial adviser explained how he worked out why he wanted to grow his practice. It was about giving his staff somewhere amazing to work, where there are opportunities for career progression and salary growth. And it was about giving his clients more support as they grew too – a level of service quality he couldn't provide as a smaller business.

Even if you're the only employee in your business, you still deserve opportunities for personal development and income growth. And your repeat clients might deserve more too.

Freelance journalist and copywriter Rachel Smith says, for her, growth is tied to earnings, in a way that looks 'more like thriving than surviving – not having to worry there isn't enough money in the account to cover expenses.'

However, earnings growth can be challenging when you're operating on your own. Even if you're very good at what you do, you'll eventually hit a ceiling on what you can earn. Whether you charge by the hour or for value, it still takes time to do the work.

You can focus on higher paying work. You can find ways to do the work faster, using tech to automate certain parts or finding ways to 'rinse and repeat' certain elements. But you'll still feel like you're on a treadmill that's getting faster and faster.

Growth vs scale

That's when you need to make a decision. Is it time to get serious about growth?

Growth is about more than money. It can give your clients confidence, and give you a competitive advantage in a crowded freelancer market. It can make you more attractive to work with – whether that's recruiting staff or building a collaborative network. And it could mean you're no longer responsible for absolutely everything in your business – freeing you up to outsource or bring in the support you need.

Tech companies know the trick is to switch from growth to scale. Scaling is different to linear growth – it's where revenue growth exceeds cost growth from a financial perspective. In other words, you make more additional income than the extra expense that comes with growth.

There are plenty of business strategy books that will teach you how to scale exponentially. But the thing is, scaling works well when you have the volume to invest in tech that creates exponential efficiency. It's the momentum behind Amazon's flywheel strategy, which starts with customer obsession, uses sales volume to negotiate lower prices and invest in fast delivery – and is powered by its own cloud computing services.

This approach is less straightforward for us knowledge workers because the value of our time does not diminish with a greater volume of hours. In fact, it can feel like the opposite. I've written hundreds (possibly thousands) of thought leadership articles over 18 years, but every story is different. I can get exactly what I need out of an expert interview, but it still takes the same amount of time to think deeply about the angles and have that conversation.

From a human perspective, it's also important to understand what growth means to you personally. How does it align with your purpose? How do you feel about the risks involved? If you could design the ideal business, the one you've always wanted to work for, what would it look like?

Making growth work for you

'You need the business to work for you, not the other way around,' a business coach once told me. That's what good growth really means – it's growth that keeps you in the driving seat. It's growth on your terms.

Maybe growth allows you to work on projects that energise you, rather than exhaust you. Or gives you enough time for the people and things that matter to you – your family, exercise, travel, or volunteering in your community. Or perhaps growth gives you enough financial security that you don't wake at night in a panic over your rent or retirement.

Whatever it looks like for you, growth also goes hand in hand with greater risk. You might need to spend more money by investing in a better website, or outsourcing business development, or taking on your first staff member. Growth strategies also demand your time and energy and take you away from billable activities.

For all these reasons, growing could mean a drop in income or investing your own funds into your business plans.

Are you comfortable doing that? Some people can afford to take that risk because they have a partner underwriting the mortgage or rent, or a comfortable cushion in the bank. Some have a stronger risk appetite.

As entrepreneurs go, I'm fairly low on the risk-taking scale. I'd seen the toll rent, staff and stock had taken on my parent's gift shop group in the early 1990s. They lost everything in the recession, like many other small business owners at the time. My husband also started building his own business straight out of university. Neither of us had the stability of a corporate paycheque to make sure the mortgage was covered.

When I met with that business coach, I felt like I was working non-stop for the business. The business wasn't working for me. I was doing everything, everywhere, all at once – still responsible for the bulk of the billable work while also managing a growing number of staff and making sure there was enough cashflow to keep paying everyone. Every time a new client brief came in, I'd have heart palpitations because I couldn't imagine how I could fit one more thing into my schedule.

We were growing, but it felt out of my control.

That's *not* good growth. Sure, it looked good in the business bank account, and everyone told me it was a 'good problem to have'. But it meant I had no time, energy or headspace for my kids, family, friends or exercise. I dreaded school holidays because the kids didn't love vacation care; they just wanted a break. And I did too. But I always felt like I was drowning in client expectations and meetings and deadlines.

I needed to reset my growth plans and make the business work for me. All those decisions were within my control.

They are in your control too.

Georgi Roberts runs a digital marketing agency called Pitstop. She has also learned what good business growth means the hard way, because at one point she was regularly working until 1 am, and then getting up at 5 am to start it all again.

She says: 'For me, good business growth is sustainable growth. It's keeping the clients I love, and scaling their revenue, and getting more clients I love. But it's also resourcing the business well, because good business growth is not working my arse off even more.'

For Georgi, good business growth also means 'taking a punt on bringing on more people'.

It means covering her baseline operating expenses with recurring revenue – in her case, social media and SEO management services. 'Then all the interesting strategic projects are the cream on top, and we can be more choosy about who we work with or how we price them,' she says.

That sounds like a great way to feel more in control to me.

Five ways to get growth right

If you haven't yet embarked on growth, you are about to turn the page on a clean new chapter where everything is possible. And you can avoid these five common missteps. If you're feeling like you're in a 'bad growth' spiral at any point, step back and think about what you can do differently.

1. **Do you need to reset client expectations?** Even though I'd taken on more experienced writers, many long-term clients still wanted me to be 'their' writer. That was no longer realistic, so we had to build their trust in the team.

2. **Do you understand the financial levers in your business?** If you don't love spreadsheets, find a bookkeeper or accountant who can set up a breakeven model for you (we'll go into this enlightening tool in chapter 7). Once you factor in annual leave and a realistic split between billable and non-billable time, you may realise you are not charging enough to cover costs.

3. **Do you know who your ideal clients are?** This little bit of analysis is a gamechanger. Make a list of all your regular or recent clients, and label them green, orange or red:
   - *Green clients* are the ones you love working with – there's a relationship based on mutual respect, they value your time and pay accordingly, the work is interesting and offers the chance to learn something new, and you can see the positive impact of what you do together.
   - *Orange clients* have the potential to be green but something is missing. Maybe their briefs are vague, or they aren't clear with feedback, or their budget is small. But the work gives you a sense of purpose.
   - *Red clients* are the ones who lowball the budget, expect things overnight, and don't value your expertise.
   Let the red clients go, and stop taking on clients who fit that profile. That will give you more time to focus your energy on the green clients, and set clear expectations and processes for the orange clients.[17]

4. **Can you delegate more?** For far too long I kept thinking it would be easier for me to just do it myself. I had to learn to let that go and accept that the time it took to train someone would pay off. I had to trust in my team.

5. **Can you set boundaries on your time?** Time management is a superpower for freelancers and consultants. It's very hard to say 'no' if your instinct is to be easy to work with. But you need to be intentional with every valuable minute of your day. Block out your calendar for the things that matter. Be unavailable. Experiment with nine-day fortnights, or starting and finishing your day earlier. Make your business work for you.

---

[17] Handy hint: don't ever let your clients see this system!

How to take your value seriously

Good growth means your business is working for you and not the other way round. And there's just one more thing you need to do to make that happen.

Set a financial target.

I am surprised by the number of freelancers and consultants I speak with who don't set an annual income target. They take the work that comes, they have good years and bad years, they pay themselves what they earn.

That makes it easy to avoid being disappointed, I guess. But it does not put you in control of your business - or your life. Imagine getting into a car with no destination in mind, and just seeing where the road takes you. All the micro-decisions you make at every turn will affect where you end up - but you have no way of knowing whether that's the most efficient or scenic route.

Whether you plan to stay working solo or build a team, you need to hold yourself accountable to something. If you don't know what you're working towards, you will never stretch yourself.

It can just be a number you put out to the universe. Once you write it down, it becomes an intention. And you can work towards making it happen.

 TAKE ACTION

To work out your *enough*, start with your ideal target income. Add in the costs of running your own business and then a profit margin. For consultancies, a profit margin of 10% to 20% is a solid target - but there are no hard-and-fast rules.

One accounting firm in Australia suggests the traditional model is a rule of three: for every dollar you pay yourself, one dollar goes to business overheads and expenses, and one dollar goes to profit.[18] But in my experience, wage costs – even if it's just you – should far exceed your overheads, even allowing for tax.

Now work out what the next one, three and maybe five years might look like. That's the growth part. Rapid growth doesn't happen overnight.

So how much growth is *enough*?

Benchmark data suggests a good organic growth goal is around 10% to 15% per year – that's growth through your own efforts, rather than by the shortcut route of acquiring another business.

However, the reality is often a bit more challenging. On average, Australia's small businesses grew revenue by 6% year on year to September 2023, according to software platform Xero.[19]

As we've established, good growth is growth that works for you. So that number could be closer to zero as long as you feel secure financially.

> If you'd stuck it out in that nine-to-five, you'd expect a modest pay rise every year. You deserve that as a business owner too.

Now you know your ideal target income, you need to start paying yourself that. Set up a separate bank account for your business if you don't have one already. Write yourself an employment agreement. Give yourself paid annual leave, in line

---

18 'How to Run a Profitable Creative Agency', Generate, 2023.
19 Xero Small Business Index (XSBI), July through September 2023.

with statutory requirements in your country – if you're not sure what they are, check with your accountant or find them online.

Welcome to the best of both worlds. Freedom to run your own show, stability of a regular paycheque. Don't stress too much over being accountable to yourself for payroll: if there's a month where cashflow is tight, that's a loan from you to the business. You can always pay yourself back.

Doing all this will force you to take yourself and your value seriously. And that's a really important step in getting the most from your own business. It also gives you some predictability for your personal finances, which can be very helpful if you ever need to ask the bank for a loan.

Defining *enough* as an end game

So far, I've focused on *enough* in the here and now: how much income you need, how much you want that to grow next year.

But what about when *you've* had enough?

One day, you'll walk out the (digital or physical) door of your business for the last time. Will you take enough with you to make it all worthwhile? What is the *enough* amount you need to move into your encore career, or even retirement?

That might feel very far off to you right now. Let's say it's 20 years – which is a very long time to run a business, trust me. Picture yourself in 20 years' time. What would you like to be doing? How much income will you need to make that happen comfortably? Let's imagine a big pot of money could create a decent chunk of that income – how much would it need to be?

That number is what you want your business to be worth in 20 years' time. Now you can work backwards to get there.

In chapter 11, I'll take you through some realistic exit strategies that could work for you.

What happens if your growth plan stalls?

Being intentional about growth and striving towards a number may be a gamechanger, but it doesn't guarantee growth. There have been months in my business when the pipeline dried up. When budgets got slashed, or the big project we were counting on was cancelled. Sometimes more than one job was iced at once, shaking any sense of complacency. Watching your business bank balance dwindle isn't much fun.

I started Writers in 2007, one month into the Global Financial Crisis. My business has been through pandemic lockdowns and post-pandemic tightening.

I've learned to use any downtime to sow some seeds for the next harvest. We always have more ideas than time, so a lull is the ideal opportunity to test a new marketing initiative. As long as we resist the urge to panic, cut rates or chase work that doesn't align with our ideal client profile.

In April 2020, when projects froze as the first COVID lockdowns were announced, I ran free webinars on writing with empathy. Whenever a client told us they'd been made redundant, we offered to help by writing their LinkedIn profiles. We did this because it was the right thing to do, but it also helped us stay top of mind when things picked up again.

Cashflow peaks and troughs are inevitable. Don't take them personally. Just have a Plan B ready to go and a healthy safety net in the bank.

What happens if your growth plan gets turbocharged?

You may get to a point where you feel like you're growing too fast. It is very unhelpful when friends tell you that's a good problem to have. Because unless you have the right model, people and processes in place to deal with a surge in demand, you will burn out. Or you'll let your clients down with a poor experience. Or both.

I'll take you through a bunch of strategies and models you can have ready to deploy in this situation. But it's best to start with a mindset shift. What worked for you in the past – hard work and talent – may not be enough to get you to the next stage of success, regardless of how you define your *enough*.

You could describe it as shifting from 'lone wolf' to 'leader'. Or you could see it as a growth mindset: believing you can turn challenges into opportunities or learn from setbacks.

Amy Ragland says she has to consciously remind herself to appreciate the opportunities that growth brings: 'Growth is hard, but it's good for us. At the end of the day, I'm the one calling the shots and making the decisions. It's easy to get stuck on the clients we didn't get or mistakes we made, but I feel lucky I get to do this freelancing thing. I can bring in a healthy income while still having plenty of time for my family.'

You can aspire to be great and still stay small. You can have the best of both worlds – the structure and people to enable good growth, without all the toxic politics and soul-crushing red-tape of a corporate giant.

All it takes is a good growth mindset.

Once you know what your *enough* is, and you have the mindset ready to work towards that goal, you have options. There are so many different ways to grow, and in the following chapters, we'll explore them all.

But first it's important to create a strong foundation. Over the years, I've realised there are five essential ingredients for a sustainable business model – whether you're working solo or bringing more people on the journey.

These five things aren't nice-to-haves, they're must-haves. They have the potential to fix any underlying issues you have right now, so those cracks don't widen as you grow. And they will set you up for a much more enjoyable journey.

The next chapter is your chance to benchmark your business in these five critical areas. *Ready?*

LET'S GROW

Are you feeling good about growing your business? Capture a few thoughts now.

1. What does good growth mean to you? How will you know when it's *enough*?

   ....
   ....
   ....
   ....
   ....
   ....
   ....

2. Why do you want to grow?

   ....
   ....
   ....
   ....
   ....

3. What excites you most about growing your business? What scares you?

   ....
   ....

....

....

....

....

....

4. Thinking about the next year, write down a target income for your business. Be real: no one is going to fire you if you don't hit it.

....

....

....

....

....

....

5. Now set a stretch target and challenging target by adding a percentage to your current income target. How do these numbers make you feel?

....

....

....

....

....

....

Every great business is clear on these five things. Whether you're a company of one or many, you can do this too.

4: The Five Ps powering good growth

The foundation for every business growth model

As we've already touched on, good growth starts with defining what is *enough* for you. What thriving looks like, not just surviving. Think of it as a circle which can expand as much as you feel comfortable. The outer boundary is your defined growth zone, where you feel you can thrive.

There are five essential elements that allow you to expand sustainably and feel in control. These make up a strong and stable business foundation, no matter what size you are. I call them the Five Ps: Purpose, Proposition, People, Processes and Profit.

Give each one equal weight and consideration. If one aspect is weak, it's much harder to reach that elusive *enough*. Without a genuine purpose or value proposition, for example, you might struggle to attract the right people. That in turn will impact your profit. Without the systems to simplify processes or free up more time, you could be hindering both your people and your profit.

However, you can't spend all day every day focusing on five things at once. That would be madness. Especially when there's billable work to be done!

That's why this chapter is your chance to prioritise. Think about where you are right now. What can you strengthen, and what's the low-hanging fruit? There might be weeks when you'll need to sharpen your proposition – to launch your website, for example. And other times when you'll be more focused on finding, developing or managing people.

We're going to use this model to benchmark your business now, but you don't need all the answers before you start growing. Each aspect will continue to evolve as you learn and grow.

Let's take a tour of the Five Ps of Good Business Growth.

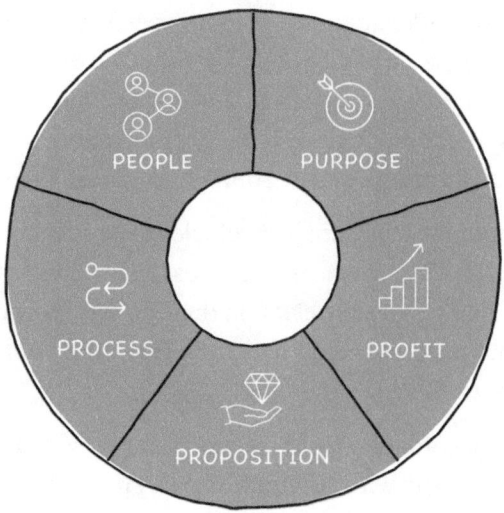

1. **Purpose** is a magnet

Does the world really need another change management consultant or web designer? Maybe not. But they do need someone who combines all the unique attributes you bring: what you care about, what you're good at, how you bring that together to do the work differently.

When you understand the ways you solve unmet needs or bring genuine value to others, it's a lot easier to get to your *enough*.

That's the power of knowing your purpose and staying true to that purpose year after year. A purpose can be a magnet for likeminded clients who will value you beyond your services, and a magnet for staff or partners who believe in the same things as you.

So, why does your business exist? Why do you do what you do? And why should anyone care?

US-based coach Ed Gandia says most freelancers start without having a clear vision of why. 'We know how to do the work. And we want more freedom and flexibility. So we might think our Big Why is freedom, flexibility, a higher income, a shorter work week, creative variety, or something along those lines,' he says.

'But that's not it. Those are just vehicles to get the outcome we truly want. The Big Why is the core reason we do what we do. And if you don't get really clear on that Big Why before you start scaling, your business could become a treadmill – not a path to true satisfaction.'

Web designer Jordanne Collins found her Big Why once she started connecting with community. She started her solo-from-home business during the pandemic and admits everything felt virtual: 'I never met people in real life, I just sat on my laptop all day and made things happen. It was like playing *The Sims*.'

When she began talking to other women doing similar things, they gave her confidence she was on the right track. That led her to focus her web services on helping female founders.

'These are the best clients for me, because the process of building the website involves guiding them through their brand strategy, identity and messaging. It creates a transformation, not just in their business but in themselves,' she says. 'They start taking themselves more seriously.'

Jordanne's purpose is to empower female service providers through design, so they can grow their own businesses and confidence.

At Writers, it took us over a decade to evolve many ideas into one succinct statement that everyone in the team believed in and could remember. Eventually, we landed on 'to help people turn their ideas into action and impact'. We don't just write for the sake of it. Generative AI can put one word after the other, but it can't get those words into the minds of real people in a way that is persuasive, compelling or relatable.

Your purpose can be BIG and aspirational. But it can also be simple, clear and actionable. And it needs to show how what you do makes a difference to others.

 TAKE ACTION

Ask yourself these questions to explore your purpose:
1. What difference do I make to my clients, or to others?
2. If I didn't do what I do, what would they miss?
3. When I feel energised at work, what is behind that?
4. Thinking back to when I first wanted to work in this field, what inspired me?

When I first signed up for a copywriting course, it was the mid-2000s, and there was already a deluge of mediocre digital content flooding our browsers and inboxes. I remember thinking *I could write that better*. So quality – and in turn, impact and action – became my purpose.

Once you have your purpose statement, the next step is to work out your values as a business. These describe what is most important to you and how you like to work – and, in line with your purpose, will guide the way you make decisions.

For example, to serve our purpose at Writers, we are **strategic** and **responsive** to achieve action and impact. We are also

curious about our clients' ideas and prepared to work **collaboratively**. We **care** deeply about the work and the people involved at every step.

Janine Pares, founder of Thinksmart Marketing, says her ambition has always been to think like an in-house marketer.

'I know what it's like on the other side, and how frustrating it is to work with agencies who just want to push the big idea. They don't understand it won't work commercially, it will never get sold internally, it's not actionable,' she explains. 'I think that sets our work apart, and helps build confidence very quickly with clients.'

Janine's purpose is to create and execute problem-solving strategies that will get the job done. And her team's values include always seeing things from the client's point of view.

We'll explore how to find *your* values in the next chapter, so you can create an awesome workplace culture. Even if it's a culture of one.

2. **Proposition** sets you apart

In the previous chapter, we talked about working out who your ideal clients are. Now it's time to flip that thinking.

Why are you ideal to them?

What do you do that no one else does? How does that add value to your clients?

That's your value proposition: a simple statement that defines the value you promise to deliver to clients. If you haven't already guessed, your purpose should give you a good starting point for a client value proposition. For example, Jordanne's proposition is more than what she does *(web design)*, it's how she does it *(website in a week)* and the impact that has for her client's businesses *(growth with confidence)*.

If you're not sure exactly how you add value to your clients, ask them. You may find the answers surprise you. It might be less about your decades of experience and more that they know you'll never let them down, which in turn makes them look good in front of their boss.

For example, until we surveyed our clients, we didn't realise how much they loved our peer review process, where every draft is reviewed by another writer who is close to the brief. That means they get a great first draft – which saves them time. It also shows how much, as a team, we care about the quality and impact of our work.[20]

You may think clients make decisions based on track record, or expertise in their sector or business, or price. But the truth is probably more emotional than rational.

We all want to work with people who are easy to work with. Maybe because they bring energy and enthusiasm, or they don't treat us like one of a hundred clients.

We also value working with people who dig deeper to solve our problems. That might show up as someone who thinks outside the brief, or challenges our assumptions.

---

[20] To keep that benefit top of mind, we added the editor's name to our work template. A simple process hack that also reinforces our proposition every time a client reads their draft.

When I asked a client recently what matters most to her, she said it's never just one thing.

'I think the fit is really important,' she explained. 'Do we vibe, for want of a better phrase? It's also a level of client care: I appreciate I'm not the only client, but I don't want to feel like I'm one of a million. I also want to work with people I can have really honest conversations with, because feedback goes both ways. I want to feel like we're on the same page, we understand each other, there's a level of respect there. And in a bonus scenario, we actually like each other.'

That doesn't sound like too much to ask. In fact, it sounds like the basis for a really healthy long-term working relationship.

 TAKE ACTION

Answer these questions to unpack your client value proposition. Ask a few different clients, and look for patterns in their responses.

1. What challenges or problems do your clients face that your services address or solve?

   ....

   ....

   ....

2. What opportunities do they have that your services help them make the most of?

   ....

   ....

   ....

3. Why do your best clients prefer working with you over their alternatives? *(Alternatives might include doing it themselves or using AI – not just other freelancers.)*

   ....

   ....

   ....

4. What are some tangible results or positive impacts your clients experience by working with you?

   ....

   ....

   ....

5. In what ways do you go beyond expectations, or how is your experience different to alternatives?

   ....

   ....

   ....

Here are some examples of common threads you might find when you ask clients why they choose to work with you:

Expertise:
- There isn't a steep learning curve to get you up to speed.
- You add long-term value.
- You can get it done faster, without my oversight.
- Your work is of high quality.

Client knowledge:
- You already know us so well, you can read my mind.
- You have access to our resources and experts.

- You understand our customers intimately.
- You have a proven track record with us.

Efficiency:
- Your processes make it easy for me.
- There are never any hassles or friction with you.
- You're clear in your communication.
- You set expectations and often exceed them.
- You manage projects seamlessly.

Positive traits:
- You take personal responsibility for issues.
- You keep your promises and meet deadlines.
- You fill us with confidence.
- You build trust with our senior team.
- You make things simple.
- You make things fun.

Now, go back to your purpose. Hopefully, the way clients want to work with you aligns with how you like to work and what you stand for.

Once you have a clear idea of your client value proposition, write it in your clients' language. Don't be afraid to use the words they give you; that's what makes your marketing feel genuine and relatable. Make this message loud and clear on your website, proposal templates, social media pages – everything you share externally.

If you're planning to take on staff, you should also think about your employee value proposition. That sums up all the reasons anyone would want to work with you. It's the vibe of your workplace, the opportunities you provide, the type of work on offer, the tech and processes. We'll go into that in more detail in chapter 5.

3. People make it all happen

Businesses of every size and shape are built on relationships. It's all about who we know and who knows us.

Clients

There are many different types of people you will depend on for growth. Let's start with clients, because without these people you have no revenue.

Not all clients are equal. Nurturing the right clients is the key to fulfilling and profitable work. These are the clients who value your services, and – when satisfied – become an unpaid salesforce as brand advocates. When you have strong, long-term relationships based on trust and mutual success, everything else is easier.

> Like attracts like. Every consistently awesome client of mine came through a warm introduction – from someone else who was great to work with.

Once you know your purpose and proposition, you will find it easier to identify (and attract) more ideal clients.

Here are three questions to ask yourself before committing to a proposal or quote with a potential new client:

- **Are they aligned with our values?** For example, one of our values at Writers is to be strategic. That means our clients need to give us a clear brief with defined objectives, value the effort and skills involved, and be open to our recommendations. If we are responsive to their needs, we expect the same in return – especially when we ask for more information or feedback.

- **Are they prepared to invest in growth?** There's a certain amount of budget they need to be able to spend to make it worthwhile for you to learn about their business or needs.
- **Are they willing to be a long-term partner?** You might want to set expectations that this could be an ongoing partnership, not a one-off transaction, if they're happy with your work.

When it comes to clients, aim for quality over quantity: it's easier to work with five ideal clients on 25 projects each in a year than 100 different clients with differing expectations and maturity. If that sounds challenging for your service model – maybe you specialise in one-off gigs – we'll explore recurring client work more in chapter 7.

Your team

Now, let's consider the people you will need to help you get all that client work done. You can outsource certain tasks to them as freelancers or fractional consultants (as we explore in chapter 6). You can employ them directly (which we'll discuss in chapter 7). Or you can partner with them in a strategic collective (see chapter 8).

Regardless of how you work with them, bringing the right people into your business matters. The quality of your work and client experience depends on it – and it will also impact your productivity, workload and wellbeing, for better or worse.

That's why it's important to think beyond the skills you need to fill to the traits and behaviours you need them to bring. For example, you probably want 'doers', not 'gunnas' – gunnas are the people who talk a good game but never quite get around to implementation.

Making a bad hiring decision can undermine confidence in your services and has a toxic ripple effect on the rest of the team. I can guarantee you'll spend sleepless nights working out how to extract yourself from that situation, especially if you're the one doing all the work because the gunna didn't get around to it.

Organisational psychologist Adam Grant says it's important to hire 'givers' – people who are instinctively generous and helpful – and weed out the 'takers'. His research found the negative impact of one taker on a team is usually double or triple the positive impact of one giver.[21]

Givers make their organisations better. Takers destroy your collective potential.

There's a saying that the sum of the parts is greater than the whole. That's what collaborating with the right people should feel like. When everyone brings a different perspective, a dynamic energy and the ability to get things done, the result is so much better than you could have achieved on your own.

4. Processes give you back your time

Every day in your business, you do dozens of small tasks that are broadly repeatable – starting a new project document, writing a proposal, responding to a client request, sending an invoice.

---

21 'Are You a Giver or a Taker?', Adam Grant, TED@IBM November 2016, https://www.ted.com/talks/adam_grant_are_you_a_giver_or_a_taker?subtitle=en.

The secret to growing beyond the hours you have in any given day is to make every single one of those micro-tasks more efficient.

Web designer Jordanne Collins has documented everything she does as a checklist, process or even video tutorial. This has made it much easier to outsource certain steps to a new admin assistant – and it also enabled her to share those videos as part of her DIY website product.

There's another good reason to get serious about your processes. If you're taking longer than you thought to do the work, it's not the client's fault. It's your processes.

If you've ever had challenging feedback and thought, *well, they didn't know what they wanted to begin with*, that's also on you. They're paying you to guide them through the project, not the other way around.

 TAKE ACTION

For the next week, write down every small step you take to get to the next stage in any given task.

Writing down every micro-step sounds tedious. But it will be worth it. You can then find opportunities to create:

- **checklists** – such as for starting a new brief, onboarding a client, reviewing work quality, or a specific task

- **templates** – such as briefing Q&As, proposals, project documents, invoices, presentations and workshops
- **policies** – such as terms of work, non-disclosure agreements, payments, employment
- **cheat sheets** – boilerplate copy for standard email responses, proposals or workshops
- **video instructions** – for specific project tasks you'd like to outsource or teach.

You can then set up systems to manage all these different processes, including tech platforms to help you automate and streamline as much as possible. We'll look at some must-haves in chapters 6 and 7.

5. Profit keeps you growing

Profit is the amount of money you have left after getting paid, and then paying all your expenses. Include your salary, super or pension contributions, and annual leave entitlements in those expenses.

If you're a creative who's been raised to think of 'profit' as a dirty word, I want you to take a big deep breath and repeat after me:

> If you're not making a profit, you're going broke.

Profit is the amount of money you will pay tax on. If you're paying taxes, you're doing something right. Peter Fuller, founder of multigenerational brand communication agency Fuller, says being purpose-driven and being profitable can – and should – go hand in hand.

'The main measure of growth is profit,' he says. 'Without profit, you really don't have a business: it's the important return on your hard work, after you take away all the costs.'

He says one of the first things he learned from his accountant is that it's good to pay tax.

'If you try too hard to maximise your tax deductibles, you're just spending money you don't have. You might not pay tax, but you're also going broke,' he says.

Profit is the amount of money you can invest back into the business to keep growing it. It allows you to launch a new website, hire a virtual assistant or in-house sidekick, or even buy your premises. Without having to put your own house on the line.

You can even pay yourself a bonus or dividend out of your net profit. Ka-ching!

Profit is a good thing, and it should be the outcome if you get the four other Ps right.

Pricing, the P driving profit

Here's another myth I'm prepared to pop: a 100% quote conversion rate is a sign of success.

If your prices aren't turning some people away, you're undercharging. So let's take a look at how you could optimise your pricing for profit.

There are typically three ways freelancers and consultants can charge for their services, and these also underpin every growth model we'll explore in the next few chapters.

- **Hourly rates:** If you charge by the hour, you're not profiting on your X factor. With your experience, you might take half the time to solve a problem compared to a newbie, but your client gets all the upside of that expertise. Your earning ability is also capped by the number of hours you're prepared to work. However, you're passing the project risk on to the client – if they drag their heels on 27 revisions, you still get paid for the work that takes.

- **Fixed project fee:** With a flat fee for a project, you can effectively make more per hour by working more efficiently. However, you take on the project risk – it's on you to define the scope upfront and charge more if the client changes their mind. Your processes can make or break this model. If you're inaccurate with your estimate, you'll pay for it with your own time. Unfortunately, I've seen this happen more often than not.
- **Charging for value:** Here, you need to be clear on the impact of your solution. What is it really worth to your client? You might come up with a genius tagline for a big campaign while you're in the shower – but do you charge your client for five minutes, or for the value of solving that high-stakes challenge? This is where strategic work and consultancy should live. You can charge for your aptitude (such as smart thinking, or analytical detail orientation) as well as your skills.

What's *your* pricing model? If you want to switch to a fixed fee for time or value, set up a spreadsheet and write down all the different services you provide. Next to that, enter a fee based on time – check how long each service takes you on average, and multiply it by your hourly rate.

Now work out what the potential value might be to your client. This might be based on how much time you're saving them, what you know a larger agency would charge, or the value of the impact it will create. For example, if my property campaign brochure needs to sell 10 luxury apartments at $10 million each, that developer needs to value the work I'm doing accordingly.

This becomes your rates sheet. You don't need to share it with your clients, but it will save you a lot of time with every quote. It also draws a line in the sand, making sure you're charging consistently. If you're tempted to under-quote because you like to work with a specific client – or if you feel under pressure to drop your fee because the client is a hard-nosed negotiator – go back to your rates sheet and stick to the numbers.

One last thing: don't set your rates lower because you're 'just' a freelancer. Freelance copywriter Steph Sta Maria says she's unapologetic about charging the same rates as a creative agency. 'I'm shocked how many people think a freelancer should be a cheaper alternative,' she tells me. She's learned to spot clients who want the best quality at the cheapest rate – and walk away.

Pack your Five Ps for your growth journey

The Five Ps give you everything you need to navigate your business through your chosen road to growth.

Think of your **proposition** as the vehicle – without it, you're not going anywhere. Your **purpose** is your GPS, helping you make the right choice at each turning point. Your **processes** are the dashboard controls, and your **profit** fuels your momentum. And the **people**? They're who you choose to bring along on the journey.

So, let's start revving that engine and look at how all these things interplay to create the ideal culture for your growing business – a workplace vibe that makes it worth coming to work, and a way of working that clients won't be able to resist.

ARE YOU READY TO GROW?

Before we begin exploring the many different growth paths now available to you, let's take a quick reality check.

Here are the five non-negotiables before you grow:

1. **Purpose:** Are you clear about why you want to grow and what that means to you personally?
2. **Proposition:** Can you explain the difference you make to your clients, or what sets you apart?
3. **Process:** Do you have a system for tracking and managing time, and templates to make the work easier and faster?
4. **People:** Who is your ideal client? And what are the skills and traits you need most in your team or partners?
5. **Profit:** Do you have three to six months of operating expenses (including your income) in your business bank account? This is your growth safety net.

LET'S GROW

Before you take the next exciting steps, jot down your initial thoughts on your Five Ps.

1. What is your **Purpose**?

   ....
   ....
   ....
   ....
   ....
   ....

2. What is your **Proposition**?

   ....
   ....
   ....
   ....
   ....

3. What are the first roles you might need **People** to help with?

   ....
   ....
   ....

4. What are the first few **Processes** you could put in place?

5. What pricing model will you use to deliver **Profit**?

A strong culture and strong values. That's how you build genuine, bullet-proof value into your business.

5: Beyond solo to culture-led growth: build your ideal business

Build the business you'd drop everything to work for

Business culture may sound like an abstract idea that's hard to measure. Yet big business leaders acknowledge it's the most underrated factor behind their company's current and future success.

Nearly two-thirds of the World's Most Admired Companies (around 600 organisations) attribute 30% of their company's market value to its culture.[22] That's a significant amount of money, given these are the highest-revenue, top-rated companies in the world.

If you've ever worked for a big corporation, you'll know there are entire teams devoted to defining, developing and measuring employee experience. Despite this, there can be a big disconnect between what a company says it stands for and what working there is really like.

Such a disconnect could well be the reason you opted out and started freelancing.

Here's the good news. As an independent consultant or freelancer, you get to define the culture of your business. As we saw in the last few chapters, being clear about what you stand for is important, even when it's an employee experience for one.

You also have the freedom – and the responsibility – to protect and evolve that culture as you grow. Best of all, it's much easier to walk the talk on your culture when you're small. Those global business leaders would no doubt agree.

---

22 'How the World's Most Admired are Shaping Culture', Korn Ferry, 2023.

What *is* culture?

Great workplace cultures are, quite simply, places where people like coming to work. It can be defined as:

- the ways those people behave
- the attitudes and beliefs that inform those behaviours
- team expectations and standards
- the experience people have every day where they work
- the technology, equipment, training and support that enables them to do their best work
- the relationships they build
- the way decisions are made
- whether they feel valued.

Culture is basically the vibe of your business. It's the sum total of all the big things, like how you define and manage flexible work hours. And lots of little things. Like giving everyone their birthday off.

The benefits of a small but mighty culture

Big businesses are focused on culture, even if they don't always get it right. But it matters for small and growing businesses like yours too.

A positive company culture is the heart of your business, and it can help you build your reputation in the market. It sets the tone for how you work with clients and other partners. It helps you feel more engaged at work, which leads to better productivity – in turn, improving customer loyalty, and creating more reasons for them to be your best advocates or refer you.

If you're thinking about hiring someone to help you, a good workplace culture will attract the right people and help you work out if they're the right fit. It can be the deciding factor if a great candidate is weighing up working with your small business against a higher paying big-business gig.

> 56% of workers say a good workplace culture is more important than salary for job satisfaction.[23]

I've experienced this firsthand, having made offers to several amazingly talented writers who could probably make more in a big consulting firm or in the comms department of a listed company. However, we've been able to tip the scales in our favour by being very clear in what we offer and how we work. We also make sure that includes things that are meaningful to the people we want in our business.

To be clear, this doesn't mean paying below market rates. It's about being thoughtful with the 'more than money' extras that add up to a better experience at work.

In my business, those things include:

- **True flexibility:** We can all work in our creative studio or from home (or a holiday house, or mum's house). We can also work the hours that suit us – including compressed work weeks (like nine-day fortnights) and part-time hours. As long as it works for the team and our clients, all options are on the table.

---

23 Glassdoor Survey, 2019.

- **Collaboration:** Another writer will read, edit and improve all work. This is a rare combination of constructive support and inner-critic counselling that makes every first draft less painful. It also helps us learn from different approaches to a brief.
- **Wellbeing budget:** Everyone gets $400 a year to spend on their physical, mental or creative wellbeing. It's not a lot, but it's a feelgood bonus when you decide you need a new pair of running shoes, or want to try Pilates or pottery, or sign up for a meditation app.
- **Curiosity budget:** Everyone gets $800 a year to spend on a training course that interests them and will help them grow. We can stretch that budget if we identify a gap in their skills that will also make a difference to the business.
- **Birthday leave:** Probably our most popular bonus – everyone gets their birthday off. Plus, someone will bake them a cake.
- **Care and support:** Everyone has your back. Someone is always ready to step in if there's a sticky problem, and we have a strict 'no dickhead' policy when it comes to clients.

Culture may feel abstract, but it comes alive every day in the way you work. It creates the right environment for you and your team to thrive and grow in a way that feels natural.

Just like nurturing the soil in a regenerative farming model.

Defining your culture

A positive workplace culture doesn't just start with a wishlist. It needs to be grounded in *your* purpose and values – what works for my business may not work for yours.

We've already talked about purpose as one of the Five Ps powering good business growth, and how to figure out your Big Why. Now it's time to focus on your values as a business.

Values describe what is most important to you and how you like to work. If your business is just you, these are likely to be the same as your personal values – how you like to live your life and what drives your decisions.

When you combine the values within your culture with all the tangible benefits you offer potential staff or contractors, you have an employee value proposition (EVP). Just like your client proposition, this is the promise you make to your people.

Again, that EVP could be just for you. Why not? In a company of one, you're the most valuable team player in the business.

Here's an example of how that plays out. Being responsive and strategic are both values at Writers. We're a high-performing team, and that may mean making hard (and fast) decisions if there's a weak link in the chain. We measure and manage productivity and always look for ways to work smarter. One client described us as 'relentless connectors' in the way we bring ideas and people together.

Some people might run a mile at the pressure of being relentless, and that's fair. You can't be all things to all people. You just need to be true to yourself.

Here's how to work out what that means for you.

1. Define your values

Values might feel like an abstract idea, but they have a very tangible impact on how you run your business and make decisions. Think back to the big turning points in your business journey. Why did you make the choices you made? What was most important to you in that moment?

I've listed some thought starters below. Be honest with yourself – don't choose a word just because you think you 'should'. There are no wrong answers. And the possibilities are vast, so if the word you're looking for isn't here, that's okay – trust your instincts and add it to your list.

Values that define performance:
- accountability
- commitment
- connection
- growth
- initiative
- perseverance
- reliability
- responsibility.

Values that define how you work:
- adaptability
- authenticity
- collaboration
- creativity
- curiosity
- efficiency
- fun
- inclusion
- learning
- making a difference
- teamwork.

Values that define how you live:
- balance
- caring
- community
- freedom
- security
- simplicity
- wellbeing.

Values that define who you are:
- belonging
- courage
- generosity
- independence
- integrity
- loyalty
- risk-taking.

Avoid overused words like 'honesty' or 'innovation'. If honesty is important to you (and really, should you be running a business if it isn't?), think about what that means when you're at your best – is it about being open and direct, or standing for fairness and justice? Similarly, innovation could mean many different things – are you a pioneer, or a creative thinker, or do your best ideas come from collaboration? Try to be specific.

Once you've listed a set of values – ideally three to four, and no more than six – think about what unites them. How would you define your culture in one sentence? For example, eyeglass retailer Warby Parker's is to 'create an environment where employees can think big, have fun, and do good'.

2. Set goals for your culture

Australian insurance broking firm GSA describes its brand values as energetic, determined, human, surprising, and valuable.

'Boring is a word that will never be associated with GSA,' says its brand book.[24] In a fairly dull sector (apologies to all insurance brokers, but it's true), this sets the firm apart.

GSA's brand book goes one step further by explaining how everyone is accountable for maintaining those values. For example, everyone is expected to take initiative – but they also need to see ideas through.

This is important, because an EVP is a two-way agreement.

> Your culture is not just what you offer people in exchange for their time and talent but what you expect in return.

---

24 'GSA Values in Action: The Little Blue Book'.

This approach sets clear and consistent behavioural goals – for you and your team. And that's what makes your culture real. Because it's one thing to say it and another to do it every single day.

Even if you're the only person in your business, how might you keep yourself accountable for your own values? If you've identified freedom to work the way you want as a value, what boundaries will you need to put in place in your client agreements? Or, if generosity is a value, do you set aside a percentage of profits towards a local community group that aligns with your purpose?

Regardless of the type of services you provide, you are in the business of expertise. So, it's also a good idea to make personal development and growth part of your culture. Especially if you are a company of one. Without a manager to mentor or coach you, your skills could quickly become less relevant. Set a target for external training – it might be completing one course a year, or joining an association that provides regular upskilling, or allocating a budget for online courses.

3. Find ways to embed your culture into everyday work

This is the fun part. Think creatively about how you can bring your culture to life – in a way that won't break your bottom line.

For example, if one of your values is inclusion, perhaps you can offer flexibility around whether to take religious or cultural holidays as leave. In Australia, some people prefer to work Australia Day because the day has a negative meaning for them – and they can take another day off when it suits them.

If belonging matters, set up some structures to support that as you grow. Especially if you're likely to have people working remotely, whether that's other freelancers, a virtual assistant, or an in-house team. That might mean daily or weekly check-ins on video calls or messaging channels, or virtual coffee breaks, or the expectation that once a month everyone comes together in real life.

I once interviewed a financial advice firm that realised its small team was operating more like a collective of independent consultants without seeing the benefits of sharing ideas for their clients or growth. They started a weekly coffee catch-up to plan and set strategic responsibilities, and the business turbocharged its growth.

If you're looking for ways to make sure people feel valued, it's important to make that visible. We used to pop anonymous thank you notes in a jar on each desk, but now we share 'warm fuzzies' feedback from clients openly on a Slack channel. You could also go around and express gratitude at those weekly check-ins. You might be surprised to see a knock-on effect with clients – they're more likely to show respect and value your services when it becomes part of your culture.

Peter Fuller describes surprising and delighting staff and clients as your 'X factor': 'Our people value an unscheduled staff lunch, or special carer's leave. We also like to be generous to our clients with celebratory bottles of champagne when they have a success, or lunch catch-ups and Christmas gifts.'

Setting boundaries as a superpower

Regardless of your values, boundaries are essential for maintaining a healthy workplace culture. Without them, you risk exhaustion, confusion and burnout – whether you are one person or many.

I asked Amy Ragland what she does if all her client leads say yes at the same time. 'I immediately freak out,' she laughs.

Then she takes an honest look at her availability.

'I'm not too proud to go back to a client and say, "I've misjudged how much time I have open; here's what I can do".'

Amy's had that conversation with me, in fact – and I appreciated her honesty. It avoided disappointing my client at a point that would have been much harder to manage.

She also notes that her long-term repeat clients will always be a priority. 'I will always, *always* jump through hoops for them to the full extent possible.'

What makes a client that valuable? For Amy, it's the sense that they'll take care of her – she never has to chase payments, and they're just good people to work with.

Amy describes this as avoiding clients who want to treat her like an employee or won't listen to her advice. 'They're hiring me for my expertise, so it's frustrating when they don't take it.'

Being honest about these things can help you identify potential red flags in a new client or project.

 TAKE ACTION

Write your boundaries down and stick them on a wall. Remember them when you get that call from another tyre kicker looking for cheap work, fast.

Here are a few red-flag thought starters.

Does the prospect sound needy or demanding?
- [ ] Won't put time into a brief
- [ ] Takes you for granted
- [ ] Demands overnight turnaround / inflexible with timing
- [ ] Says they have no budget

Do they prioritise quantity over quality?
- ☐ Project scope has no meaning or impact
- ☐ Unrealistic volume of work
- ☐ Doesn't value the skill and time the work takes

Are they vague with details?
- ☐ Always has scope creep
- ☐ Doesn't have a plan or objectives
- ☐ Needs you to read their mind
- ☐ Poor/inarticulate feedback
- ☐ Unwilling to give written feedback

Like Amy, I have learned to trust my instincts over many years. But my biggest challenge is saying no. Amy puts it best:

> 'If I feel like they're good people, I'll recommend them to someone in my network. If they're jerks, I'll politely decline and let them fend for themselves.'

Benchmarking your culture

When Peter Fuller began employing staff in his brand communications agency, Fuller, he consciously set about building a better culture than the other places he'd worked – the cut-throat, authoritarian and (at the time) misogynistic world of Australian newspapers.

Purpose and values were not on the business radar 30 years ago, so Peter trusted his instincts on what a positive workplace could look like: 'Our culture was always based on values of respect and trust, joy, generosity, courage and excellence. The first 10 employees happened to all be women – I think that influence developed a culture that was more caring than if we'd been a group of testosterone-driven blokes.'

Fuller's internal caring culture and external 'for good' philosophy evolved over several decades before Peter and his team decided to benchmark their efforts. In 2021, it became the first marketing agency in Australia to achieve both B Corp and carbon neutral certification.

'This made us feel good, but was just the start of the journey,' Peter admits. 'These were very "warts and all" audits, which challenged us to do better.'

He says the process helped his team refocus on their purpose and values, and provided another point of difference for staff recruitment and retention.

Staff get involved in initiatives like 'low carbon weeks' (where they aim to reduce commuting emissions), the company's Reconciliation Action Plan and a sought-after fellowship program. Modelled on the Churchill Fellowship, this in-house-funded program gives one person the opportunity to travel and learn through a conference, study tour or research program. They can choose any subject they are interested in – so far that's included reduced carbon website builds, diversity in communications and cultural nuances in South Korean design.

For a small business, Fuller has a rock-solid platform focused on doing good. But Peter says if he was starting again, he'd begin by engaging an agency to help him establish purpose, values and beliefs, clear goals and objectives: 'In the early days, the advice we received was mainly around accounting and P&Ls. That's necessary, but it doesn't help define your point of difference, who you really are in a competitive market. It took us the first year working with several business coaches before we had established that important 'true north'.

Making sure your culture sticks as you grow

There is only one way to make sure your culture, values and purpose become a valuable foundation for your business, and that's to regularly spend time working *on* the business, not just in it.

Amy acknowledges that she often gets stuck in the day-to-day client work and forgets she's also a business owner. 'If you don't schedule time to work on your business, it will never get done, because there's more short-term gratification in working on projects that will pay you now versus projects that may pay later,' she admits.

Schedule the time in your calendar. Once a month, step back and re-evaluate your business – is it still serving your purpose? If you find it hard to keep yourself accountable on your own, ask someone you trust to be a mentor. Think of it as an advisory board of one – just sit down with them for a coffee once a month and ask them to challenge you on specific decisions you are making.

LET'S GROW

We're ready to start exploring all the options you have for growth. But first, it's time to commit to your culture on paper.

1. List your values as a business – choose three to six words to describe the behaviours you want to stand for at work.

   ....
   ....
   ....
   ....
   ....

2. Now translate those into a few tangible actions or goals. What will you hold yourself and others accountable for? What will you give your team – and what do you expect in return?

   ....
   ....
   ....
   ....
   ....

3. Describe your culture in one sentence. You can use this formula or come up with your own:

   At ...., we create an environment where everyone can ...., ... and ....

Want to scale without the salary risk? Here's how to set the right people up for success.

6: Beyond solo to hybrid: outsourcing

Start here if you're not ready to hire

When I ask most people what it would take to grow their business, they immediately picture hiring staff. That's the traditional route to building an agency-style model, but there are other ways.

You can start outsourcing certain tasks to virtual assistants or fractional consultants, or hand entire projects over to other freelancers. You're still accountable for managing their quality and paying them, but there's a lot less payroll admin and career development.

I call this the 'hybrid model'. There are no hard-and-fast rules: you can run an entire team of freelancers or supplement a smaller in-house team with specialists for specific projects. Either way, you can call yourself an agency – if labels matter to you. And you can start to get the benefits of working collaboratively: expand your services, add more versatile skills, build more capacity, say yes to more work.

But here's the thing: there is a big difference between being a freelancer and commissioning work to other freelancers. You might be surprised how often freelancers miss the mark. That can lead to more work for you – whether that's giving constructive feedback, redoing their work or realising you should have spent a lot more time upfront setting clear expectations.

In an ideal world, you'll provide recurring work to a small, trusted group of freelancers who learn, over time, what works for your clients. That might take some frustrating rounds of feedback at first – just as it would for a new in-house team member – but in theory the time you invest upfront will pay off.

I say in an ideal world because I am yet to crack that freelancer ROI. As an agency with an in-house team, we don't always have regular overflow work. And when we do, we're under the pump already.

> Finding time to thoroughly onboard and brief a new person can feel overwhelming.

A semi-fixed casual arrangement may be a good compromise, but it needs flexibility on both sides. For example, when we found an editor who made us all better writers, we set up an agreement so we could access his talents on an ad hoc basis. Fortunately, he was willing to accommodate us around his other work. His terms of work have evolved with us, from casual with guaranteed hours to casual ad hoc around his new full-time role. He's proactive and gives us endless flexibility. In return, he feels like part of a team with a strong culture and purpose.

You can't do it all

Freelance content writer Sarah Spence didn't plan to start her own agency, but as she kept saying yes to projects and built strong client relationships, her workload grew.

After landing a few major projects at once, Sarah realised she couldn't do it all. She started outsourcing part of the writing and editing to other freelancers, and slowly built a remote team across Australia.

In 2022, following some truly epic triple-digit revenue growth, she decided to bring her creative resources in-house. Just two years after hiring her first employee, her content marketing agency, Content Rebels, had 21 people employed on a permanent part-time or full-time basis, plus a pool of over 100 subcontractors.

That's a lot, and a lot of quick growth. Sarah admits some of those decisions came back to bite her: 'The talent demand was absolutely there for us to make that decision. A few of our subcontractors were keen on more consistent employment, and we wanted more control over their time. We'd also built a really beautiful culture that people wanted to be part of.'

The demand was there on the client side, too. Until it wasn't. Four major clients turned off their content marketing programs at once. In 2023, Sarah streamlined her in-house team to eight, and she now depends on 15 regular subcontractors. She says:

> 'I think the best model is to have a fantastic in-house core team and be able to scale up as needed with a fantastic subby pool. Don't forget about that pool in between jobs – they need to feel part of the culture.'

How do you make freelancers feel part of your culture when it's not financially – or geographically – realistic to extend your employee benefits to a large pool of freelancers? Sarah learned that the hard way: 'We used to invite our freelancers to join our catch-up chats after weekly team WIP meetings – which they loved because freelancing is lonely. But then they wanted to be paid for that time, which became untenable.'

Part of Content Rebel's caring culture is to allocate four 'gift days' dedicated to self-care for the in-house team. Everyone takes the same day off, so clients know the business is closed for the day and no one feels the urge to check email or Slack.

Sarah admits that gift day sometimes felt 'unaffordable' when revenue was lean, but she suspects there would have been zero productivity gain from making people work that day. It's worth remembering that when you start setting up generous culture benefits, it's very hard to wind them back.

Right people, right seats

Sarah credits *Traction* by Gino Wickman with helping her understand how to approach hiring for business growth in a 'more clinical' way.

'If you have even a smidge of "people pleaser" in you, you need to find a way to take the emotional heartache out of those decisions,' she says. 'Gino's concept of the "right people in the right seats" means first you need to work out what seats, or roles, you really need, and then whether the people you have are right for your business and in the right seats.'

I've worked with people who are absolutely right for our business – but we didn't have the right role for their skills. It's a hard decision, but you need both to make it work.

US-based Amy Ragland tells me she doesn't feel ready to hire an employee, but she is exploring other options to evolve her model. One involves a shift to becoming a general content agency, beyond the compliance-regulated niche of financial services writing.

'In that model, I'd be the person bringing in clients and doing more of the marketing. I'd have a project manager running the client work. Then a team of writers and editors would handle the actual content production,' she explains. All those people could be freelancers, paid by the hour or a fixed project fee.

This model could give Amy the flexibility she needs to respond to regular work, with a little less risk and payroll responsibility. But it still needs some careful thought around each of the Five Ps for good growth.

Let's see how the Five Ps might look for this versatile model.

Purpose

A clear and compelling purpose will draw the right freelance partners to your business. The best freelance talent tends to be busy – they might even have a waiting list. You want to be at the top of their preferred client list, and that comes down to how easy you make it to work with you.

How might your purpose make you an ideal client for your favourite partners? Here's an example. One frustration many freelancers share is they rarely get to see the impact of their hard work. They are usually removed from the final decision-making process, or they don't always get the constructive feedback to help them grow. If your purpose is all about making a tangible impact with your work, sharing that information with your hybrid team should be a natural part of your working rhythm.

Proposition

When you're operating solo but outsourcing to a remote team, you need to decide how much is 'behind the scenes' for your clients. Do you present your business as an individual or team on your website and proposals?

This is a very personal decision. Some freelancers have told me it feels disingenuous to 'pretend' they have staff, and they feel their clients want to know they'll be personally involved. They might write their website in the first person; for example, 'I'll be involved in all the work we do together, either working with you directly or managing the team I've hand-picked for you'.

Others believe profiling the entire team signals broader capacity to clients. They would write their website using 'we' and 'our', and provide bios and pics of their regular freelancer team. If you decide to go this route, make sure those people are happy to be 'white labelled' as part of your business.

Then, work out how much direct client contact you want your freelancers to have. This might depend on the type of work they do, and how strategic and valuable you consider their input – and impact:

- Should they contact clients directly with project questions?
- Will they be directly involved in discovery sessions?
- How will you introduce them? For example, 'our strategic design partner' instead of 'our Creative Director'.

People

People will make or break your hybrid model, because they are responsible for executing work on your behalf and represent your brand externally.

Choosing the right talent for the right project is a skill you'll need to develop. I've seen firsthand just how good marketing consultant Sue-Ella McDowall is at finding, nurturing and developing freelance consultants and creatives – because I was lucky enough to be one of them, and I've worked with many of her hand-selected crew over the last 15 years.

'It's nothing about skill,' she tells me when I ask her what her secret is. 'If they're still a bit shaky on skill, we can work on that.'

> 'What I'm attracted to is their personality. Are we going to get on well together? What are they going to be like in front of a client who's a bit of a dick? How do they present themselves? That's my recipe for choosing a freelancer.'

Phew. Glad I passed that test as a rookie!

So where do you find these hidden gems? You can tap your network – a warm referral to a trusted professional is a rare and precious gift. You can advertise on specialist freelance platforms. You can make it easy for people to apply to join your tribe with a simple form on your website.

When you find the right people, treasure them. Make them feel trusted and respected, part of the team. And pay them on time.

Processes

If I get frustrated because a freelancer has failed to deliver on their promise, that's partly on me and my processes. I haven't set them up for success as a remote collaborator.

Often, the biggest issue is a lack of communication – which can come from not setting clear expectations on both sides for using the appropriate channels.

Sarah Spence uses Asana for workflow project management across her agency, and everyone works collaboratively in Google Docs rather than Microsoft Word. They communicate via Slack rather than email, which she says is better for ad hoc idea sharing. Even clients are encouraged to jump onto the Slack channels.

Here are some things to consider when setting up freelancer management processes:

- Do you need to onboard them before you start your first project? Consider a welcome pack with templates, processes, and any compliance policies such as non-disclosure agreements or non-compete agreements.
- How do you brief them? What do they need to know to understand what a good outcome looks like?
- Do you give them a budget to work with, or a set number of hours at their hourly rate? If the latter, do you need them to track and share time?
- Do you need them to access your workflow management system? For example, if you use a platform like Asana, you can add them to tasks and deadlines.
- If they have direct client contact, do you set them up with an email address in your business name?
- Do you expect them to take care of client feedback? If so, how many rounds?
- How do you communicate with them: email, a dedicated Slack channel, video meetings?
- Do you want them to join your team or client work-in-progress meetings? How will you compensate them for that time?
- Do you want to include them in your business strategy meetings? How will you compensate them for the value they bring to internal initiatives?

Many of these processes are very similar to the things you'd need for an in-house team.

The difference is your freelancers see you as a client rather than a boss, and you are one of many clients to them.

So, your goal is to make it as simple as possible for them to deliver exactly what you need – and hopefully knock it out of the park.

There's one other type of team member available to you in the hybrid model, but it's more 'process' than 'people'. That's Generative AI. ChatGPT, Claude or another large learning model could take care of some of the tasks you would otherwise outsource, such as transcriptions, podcast show notes, data analysis, coding or writing social media posts.

Profit

It's just as important to make sure the breakeven model tilts in your favour when you're paying freelancers.

Consultants and freelancers are running their own business. Depending on the regulations in your market, that means they are likely to be responsible for paying their own holiday leave, tax and insurance. Superannuation or pension contributions can be a grey area, so it's a good idea to check with your accountant how freelancers or subcontractors are classified as those laws are subject to change.

Freelancers also don't need you to provide a computer or office space. And it's up to you whether you extend any employee value proposition benefits, such as team drinks or gym subsidies.

All this makes freelancers a potentially more cost-effective model in the short term – especially if your project load is unpredictable. If work gets stalled or pushed back, you're not paying them to twiddle their thumbs. However, they will, quite rightly, charge more per hour than the equivalent part-time salary rate to compensate for the unpredictable nature of your arrangement.

Our fee model is a fixed price per project, so when we use freelancers we tend to provide a budget that gives us a margin for managing the work. Sometimes we'll ask them to quote for the work to check that the rate is realistic. Over time, we've found some types of work – such as editing and proofreading – are easier to outsource and put less pressure on our margins.

Think about all the different types of billable work you do, and check your profit percentage over the past year. In general, the type of work with the highest margin will give you the most wiggle room to outsource.

And how much margin should you be making on your freelancer rates? As a rule of thumb, at least 25% and ideally 50%. You're the one bringing in the work, managing the client relationship and timelines, wrangling any feedback and waiting for that invoice to be paid.

To outsource or not to outsource?

Let's sum up the pros and cons of the flexible hybrid model.

In the pro-freelancer corner, we have:

- **Flexibility:** Scale your team up or down depending on the project scope and timeframe. That means you can take on more work with less risk, because if a job falls through or the client moves on, you won't be stuck with underutilised staff.
- **Fresh perspectives:** Plug any skill or expertise gaps in your offering with a specialist in that area. You'll also gain broader insights into the client's challenges.
- **Potential cost savings:** Compared with hiring in-house staff, you save on benefits, office space, equipment, tax, pension payments and insurance.
- **Reduced management time:** It should take less time to hire, onboard and pay freelancers. You also have less responsibility for managing their career development and emotional wellbeing.

And in the freelancer-fail corner, we have:

- **Inconsistent quality:** If you're churning through a rotating roster of freelancers, it takes more time to get them up to speed on the nuances of each client's needs, provide feedback and make sure the client will be happy.
- **Communication challenges:** If everyone is working remotely and across different time zones, they're less likely to ask questions, challenge assumptions or raise alternative solutions.
- **Availability issues:** You have less control over their time and commitment to your projects and priorities.
- **IP risks:** You're opening the door to your intellectual property, client contacts, ways of working and systems. That takes trust – and some robust written agreements.

Rachel Smith has two virtual assistants and also relies on freelance support to run her copywriting business, jobs database and community Rachel's List, podcast *The Content Byte* and annual event Content Byte Summit. She is one busy woman. 'I've learned one of the hardest things about having a freelance team is they have their own clients and they only belong to you for a short amount of time. Even if your brain is firing with ideas you want to action, you have to respect their time.'

She took on a consultant to sort out some serious systems to keep all the moving pieces of her work flowing. One virtual assistant handles all her social media, research and personal life admin. The other takes care of systems and newsletters. She also has an 'official wing woman', who Rachel describes as a 'Jill of all trades: sales, digital marketing, talks me off a ledge'.

'I have to trust they're doing their role with minimal input from me because they're all remote. And it really does work,' she says.

> 'My rock-solid freelance team takes care of all the stuff I used to procrastinate over for two hours, so I can take on bigger writing projects. The things I want to be working on.'

When I first started taking on staff, I found it very hard to let tasks go. Rachel says it's the same when you're running a freelance team: 'I used to be the person on Rachel's List who hoarded all the tasks and had a very ad hoc way of delegating. I thought, *Oh, no one can do that as well as I can, so I'll just stay up until midnight.*'

So what changed?

'First, I learned I can't do it all and I don't want to. I learned to be honest about what I love doing, and to outsource the rest. And I learned people will do things differently to you – but it gets done, and that's okay.'

Plus, she outsourced her system set-up. 'It is so important to have a systems-oriented person in your business, maybe a business manager, especially for a creative ideas person like me,' she admits.

Would she ever hire an in-house team as she keeps growing?

'I see the appeal of finding someone you really love working with and building something together,' she says. 'But I don't think starting an agency is for me; I'm just a lover of words, and I don't want to do the admin and the payroll and all that.'

If you feel like that too, the outsource model might be right for you. And it can be a good way to gently test the waters (and strengthen your client list) before you leap headfirst into hiring permanent staff.

We'll explore what that takes in the next chapter.

> **ARE YOU READY TO OUTSOURCE?**
>
> **The hybrid model might be right for you if:**
>
> ✓ you have a strong network of trusted freelancers or contractors
>
> ✓ your project workload is variable but defined by repeatable tasks
>
> ✓ you want to test your model before fully committing
>
> ✓ you have systems to set a remote workforce up for success
>
> ✓ your fixed project rates allow you to make a 25% to 50% margin on freelance costs.
>
> **The hybrid model might *not* be right for you if:**
>
> ✗ you do not have good communication and workflow systems
>
> ✗ you need consistent high quality without too much oversight.

LET'S GROW

1. Make a list of the internal tasks and any types of client work you *don't* love doing (or don't have the skills for but your clients want). In this list, highlight the tasks and services you could outsource.

   ....

   ....

   ....

   ....

   ....

   ....

   ....

2. Choose three of these highlighted items. How much time could you save each week if someone else took care of that item for you? What is the value of that time?

   ....

   ....

   ....

   ....

   ....

   ....

   ....

'I thought, if I get 20 hours a week back, can I make more than her salary? **I looked at it as a long-term investment. And it has paid off, 100%.**'

Jordanne Collins

7: Beyond solo to small business: the traditional growth model

Now that you're your own boss, are you ready to be the boss?

In 2013, five years after launching my freelance business, I hired a business coach. At the time, I was feeling overwhelmed. I hadn't quite figured out the need for boundaries at that time, and my innate bias towards optimism – *sure, I can fit that in* – meant I was constantly overcommitted. My heart raced so fast every time I saw another client request land in my inbox, I felt close to a panic attack.

I was outsourcing some basic admin to a virtual assistant, but I needed more help to feel more in control. Not just in control of the business, but also my life. I was teetering on the edge of chaos, with two very busy kids at primary school, and a major home renovation in my near future.

That coach helped me identify the first two roles to hire. First, I needed another writer – someone who could take care of our small business clients while I focused on the higher value corporate work that was starting to come through referrals. I had built up a small buffer of cash in my business account, and felt comfortable offering two days a week on a permanent part-time basis.

The second role was just as important. While I would have loved to clone myself, that's not a realistic hiring plan. Plus, what I really needed was someone who had different skills and motivations – who could do all the things I didn't want to do or (if I was honest) wasn't all that good at. Like having difficult conversations with clients about money, or timing, or both. Setting realistic expectations for turnarounds. Following up on paperwork and payments. Keeping clients engaged and happy while I took a proper family holiday.

We defined that role as an Accounts Relationship Manager, and through friends I found the ideal candidate: someone who'd recently been made redundant from an agency role. I offered her an hourly rate for fixed casual hours. At the time, I shared a tiny office space with a local landscape design company, and my patient Accounts Relationship Manager spent her two days a week at an Ikea desk wedged under the staircase.

Then came my next big challenge: learning how to delegate.

The confidence to lead

Before we get into the nuts and bolts of building an agency model – the financials, the processes, finding clients and all that fun stuff – I want to spend a bit of time on what it actually means to be the boss. The person where the buck stops. The one who, in the words of Simon Sinek, should be prepared to 'eat last'. Because that role is very different to freewheeling freelancing.

I'll admit I found delegating tough, even though that was the total point of taking on staff. I had a very hard time letting things go.

> I'd spent a long time building trust with my clients and had a misguided belief only I could do certain things.

I also brought a bit of emotional baggage to the task of managing others. That confidence-shaking turning point in my life, when I was fired from a job I loved, haunted me. I knew, deep down, it was partly because I hadn't effectively managed my tiny team at that time. I had operated like a lone ranger when I should have been coaching them and encouraging them to work with me on better solutions.

I didn't do a good job of setting boundaries, defining responsibilities or giving constructive feedback.

I am still working on this, decades later.

Brooke Hill felt the same when she decided to shift from subcontractors to permanent employees in her Australia-based content agency Wonderthink.

'Making that commitment has been the best thing, because it forced me to look at the stories I was telling myself about what an agency could be,' she says.

> 'I had to flip my preconceptions about how to manage people. I thought I needed to know all the answers. But it's really about enabling them to do their best work.'

Do not underestimate the courage it took Brooke to make this leap. At the time, her business revenue was declining, and the merest whiff of recession talk had clients shedding retainers and slashing budgets. But instead of paring back her model, Brooke leaned all the way in and invested in people.

'I'd always thought I'd just return to a corporate job if the business didn't work. But when things started to decline and that choice was right in front of me, I realised I love this so much. I love working with other people, I love the energy I get from that, I love my clients. I didn't want the alternative,' she says.

Brooke surrounded herself with good mentors who encouraged her. Her accountant gave her confidence in the numbers. And she focused on the one thing that will make or break your enjoyment of being the boss: hiring well.

We'll dig into that later in this chapter. But first, it's time to take a good hard look at yourself.

Redefining your role for the better

For consultants and freelancers who have spent many years becoming the best at their craft, it takes different skills (and time) to nurture the talent in others. When you evolve your company of one into a company of two, three, four or more, your role in the business will change overnight.

Here are three questions to consider before you jump in:

- How much time are you willing to spend training, coaching and mentoring others? With a team of eight, managing people might account for half my time in any given week.
- What are you prepared to let others do for you – even if their first efforts aren't quite up to scratch?
- Are you prepared to be accountable for the quality of all the work, even if you don't do it? As a leader, the buck stops with you.

On the upside, this is also your chance to redefine your role for the better:

- What are the things you do now that you really don't enjoy, like chasing invoices or writing proposals?
- What are the things you know you're not the best at? That might be asking clients for more money, setting up robust processes, or detail-oriented work like analysing data or proofreading.
- Where are the gaps in your skillset – are there things clients have asked for help with that you don't feel confident in? That could include higher value strategic work or running workshops.

The in-house staff advantage

Freelance writer Oyelola Oyetunji hasn't taken on anyone to help her yet. But she says she will if she doesn't have enough time to deliver for all her clients – and still wants to work with all of them.

'I'd like to start outsourcing some of the stuff that takes up time that I don't enjoy doing, so I can take on more clients. Things like invoicing, writing proposals and fiddly time-consuming things like social media graphics,' she tells me.

If you have run out of hours in a day to get everything done, you do need help. Effectively, you need to buy more hours from someone else's time. That can be done by outsourcing to another professional – whether that's a bookkeeper, business development manager or another freelancer.

The alternative is a more serious commitment. You can take on that person as a staff member on a permanent or casual-contract basis.

One of the most significant benefits I've found with this approach is that they are also more committed to you and your business. They are available in the hours you agree, and keen to learn and develop in line with your business model. They are willing to follow the processes you've put in place, which provides a more consistent experience for your clients.

Over time, they build valuable knowledge of those clients and develop expertise in their industries or project types.

You have opportunities to learn from your staff too. Clients tell us that our disciplined peer review process is our competitive advantage, and it's also an advantage for the team. We know someone else will make our writing better. We learn from the approach of others. And ultimately, that means a better-quality product.

So, hiring permanent staff is a commitment that goes both ways.

Brooke Hill says she immediately saw the next-level shift in her team when she pivoted from a contractor-only model.

'I get such joy out of seeing them achieve something challenging or feel rewarded by the results. I wouldn't have that in any other way of operating,' she says.

As her team works remotely, she knew it would be important to bring her core team together physically to start building trust in the culture. A three-night creative retreat was the answer. 'It was 95% about filling our creative cups and spending time with each other. A small component was devoted to how we build the culture we want to create,' she says.

Plus, Brooke has retained a pool of contractors across Australia, New Zealand and Canada. That's a 'best of both worlds' model for flexibility and 24/7 response.

Dependable commitment is one benefit of taking on permanent staff. But is there a tangible return on investment?

When web designer Jordanne Collins took on her first part-time employee, she had a clear view of the potential payoff.

'She's now working three days a week for me, turning around our "website in a week" packages,' Jordanne explains.
'I thought, *If I get 20 hours a week back, can I make more than her salary?* I looked at it as a long-term investment – I knew if she could do three or four websites a month it would pay off. And it has, 100%.'

Jordanne also found that by letting go of some of the work tasks she didn't love, she fell in love with her business again. What's not to like about that? Plus, having an employee helped her be more consistent with service delivery – and in turn, get more consistent work.

That consistency is a plus for clients. They also like the idea of knowing you're growing: it signals maturity and stability in a partner. It makes them feel like they've chosen a winning team. They may also appreciate the different perspectives you can bring as a combo. And they certainly like having someone available for last-minute urgent things – which you cannot promise as a solo consultant who is occasionally unwell, taking a break or booked up until Christmas.

There are longer term benefits too. When staff leave (and they will leave), if they've had a good experience, they will become your best advocates. Some of our alumni end up being clients.

In-house staff can also enable your succession plan, which we'll explore in chapter 11.

The hidden risks of taking on staff

The opportunity to grow through staff comes at a cost, of course. As well as paying salaries, you may have to pay annual leave, sick leave, superannuation or pension contributions, and some types of workers insurance. Those costs will depend on where you operate – in some cases, payroll tax may also apply. In Australia, I've found these 'on costs' typically add around 20% to 25% to the base salary depending on the hours a person works.

And most of that is money your staff don't see or perceive as a benefit.

You need to have enough financial stability to know you can pay these costs on time. That can be a keeping-me-awake-at-night commitment – especially if an unforeseen event like a global pandemic knocks the wind out of your project pipeline.

So money is a big factor in this decision. But just as importantly, will you find the ideal employee?

Every business leader, whether they run a company of two or 200,000, will tell you it's really hard to find good people. And even harder to keep them. Especially employees with high-demand skills. In Australia, 88% of employers say they're experiencing a skills shortage, and it's only getting worse.[25]

A tight labour market is great for freelancers looking for work. It's not so great for freelancers looking to hire an employee.

It also takes time and emotional energy to manage others. As millennials and Gen Z take over the workforce, this might become even harder. Global research suggests the younger generation – especially women under 30 – have alarmingly low resilience.[26] As their manager, it's also your job to help them reset after a difficult situation at work and develop skills to cope.

Sometimes that means having tough conversations. Not everyone will be the right fit – some people interview exceptionally well but find it harder to deliver on their confident promise. I've had to let a few people go within their probation period, and I always find that incredibly awkward – even if we both know it's for the best.

In a small team, there is no room for people who just want to go through the motions. If one person is unhappy, it has a ripple effect on everyone else.

---

25 Hays Salary Guide FY23/24.
26 2023 Global Resilience Report.

What happens if you hire someone and your best clients still only want to work with you? They've become used to having you on call; they depend on you reading their mind. And you don't want to make them unhappy.

It can be really difficult to wean clients away from depending on you. But it has to be done. A few professional consulting partners have told me they always send at least two people to any client meeting. The client benefits from more perspectives, and it builds trust in the team rather than an individual.

And finally, there is also the potential risk of losing your intellectual property or even some clients if someone leaves. Before you start to think about hiring, make sure you have a robust employment contract drawn up with requirements around data access and non-compete periods. Think of it as a pre-nup – hopefully you'll never need it, but it could save your business financially and legally in the worst-case scenario.

Who you need on board

There's a whole bunch of people working in a traditional agency, and a hefty proportion have obscure titles like 'Traffic Manager' or 'Data Ninja'.

When you're shifting from a company of one to two or three, you need versatile people who can, and are prepared to, do more than one thing. Who will thrive on variety. Who are willing to solve any problem that passes their desk – whether that's a client pushing back on scope, or the toner's run out and you need those workshop materials in an hour.

So, you probably don't need a traffic manager.

Your first hire will most likely come down to two choices:

- Someone client-facing, who can give clients the best possible experience and manage relationships while you get the work done; or
- Someone to help you get the work done – such as another writer, programmer, designer, accountant or consultant. Maybe they have similar skills to you, or maybe they have the skills you lack.

Both these options come in a few shapes and sizes.

Depending on the country you operate in, there will be a bunch of regulations and entitlements that you **must** check before making an offer. Permanent full-time and part-time employment typically come with legal entitlements – such as compulsory superannuation or pension contributions, paid annual leave, sick leave, personal or carers' leave, public holidays, health insurance and (eventually) long-service leave.

Casual employees usually aren't paid annual leave, and there's less commitment to hours. However, casual hourly rates tend to be higher than the equivalent full- or part-time salary because they're taking on that risk.

Once you've crunched some numbers on salary and hours, you're ready to write a role description. That means it's time to wheel out your employee value proposition (EVP).

What do you offer as an employer?

Beyond salary and other financial benefits, your EVP sums up all the reasons anyone would want to work with you. It's the vibe of your workplace, the opportunities you provide, the type of work on offer, the tech and the processes.

This is where all the work you did on culture in chapter 5 pays off. For example, if birthday leave is one way you'll embed your culture into everyday work, that's part of the package.

Common 'value adds' in an EVP include:

- **flexibility**, such as being able to start earlier or finish later around school runs, or choosing a compressed work week (such as working 38 hours per week over a nine-day fortnight)
- **work/life balance support**, such as a 'no questions asked' carers' leave policy or a 'work from anywhere' policy
- **physical and mental wellbeing support**, such as a wellbeing allowance, free meditation apps or funding for counselling
- **a strong sense of meaning and purpose**, which can include your family-like culture, B Corp status, or robust policies on clients or sectors you *won't* touch
- **community support**, such as aligned not-for-profits or volunteering
- regular **social events**
- funding for **external training**
- clear **career paths and opportunities** for development.

Many of these things are low cost and relatively easy for a very small business to implement. Just make sure you budget accordingly, document the policies clearly and encourage everyone to participate by making benefits visible.

For example, our team blocks out their calendars around their flexible work hours and working-from-home days. This helps us all allocate work and meetings but also reminds everyone these options are available.

Hiring well

Brooke Hill tells me everything flows from your hiring decision. So, it's pretty important to get that right. Like me, she'd previously struggled to manage an inherited team in a corporate role. This time, she had control over who would work alongside her.

It's one thing to have control over the decision, and another to make the right decision. My biggest and most costly mistakes as a business owner involve poorly planned hiring decisions. Sometimes it's because I've panicked and quickly plugged a project gap. Others, because I was too busy to pay attention to tiny red flags in the interview or reference-checking process.

A poor hire will come back to bite you in so many ways – including team morale and client experience.

So, take it slowly. Make a clear plan for who you need, their roles and responsibilities, and how you'll bring them on board so they can start doing their best work as soon as humanly possible. Allocate responsibilities: who will train, manage and mentor them? How will you give them feedback?

A 'success profile' is one way to document these issues. Think beyond a traditional job description to work out what will make that person succeed in your business. What skills do they need? What motivates them? What behavioural traits define the way they work?

This will help you sift through dozens of applications. It also helps you ask the right questions in an interview and manage expectations for performance once they're on board.

- **What are the ideal skills and behaviours you need that person to have already?** Think about what really matters. Some things, like using your workflow management system, are easy to train for. Other skills are fundamental. For example, in our business, everyone needs to be able to ... wait for it ... write well.

- **What are some traits and attributes that person needs to thrive in your business or be the person you want to work alongside?** These relate more to who they are than to what they do – and are significantly harder to change. Believe me, I've tried. Ideally, these will align with the values you established in chapter 5. Examples include being positive, proactive, and willing to jump in and help with tasks outside their job description.

- **What are some drivers that might motivate your ideal candidate? What are their interests? What will keep them engaged?** This will help you flex your EVP; for example, if work/life balance is a strong motivator, you can make your working-from-home or flexible-hour opportunity the star of your job ad.

Here's a sample success profile.

POSITION: CLIENT RELATIONSHIP MANAGER

WHAT YOU DO

Competencies	Experiences
Skills and behaviours you need to succeed	*Assignments that prepare you for future roles*
Excellent communication	Manage key client relationships
Relationship management	Identify opportunities to add value to clients
Strategic planning	Run client briefings and WIPs
Financial acumen	Write successful proposals and pitch to clients
Problem-solving	Mentor/coach a junior team member
Mentoring and coaching	Run internal strategy sessions
Identifying and implementing new tech and processes	

WHO YOU ARE

Traits	Drivers
Attributes that help you thrive	*Values and interests around your career path, motivation and engagement*
Strategic thinking	Connection
Calm under pressure	Strategic impact
Proactive problem-solver	Influence
Adaptable	Problem-solving
Empathetic	Entrepreneurial spirit
Analytical	Autonomy
Collaborative	Professional recognition
Confident	

Where will you find this person?

If you're evolving into this model from the hybrid outsourcing approach, you may already have the ideal candidate within your freelancing pool. But it's also a good idea to cast the net wider and be open to new perspectives for your business.

I once wrote a success profile and role description for the type of person I knew I really needed in my business. But it felt like I needed a unicorn – no one with all those skills existed, surely? So I phoned my friend Renee. You might remember, she was the one who encouraged me to get into this whole copywriting business in the first place. She also has an uncanny knack for spotting hidden potential in people, coaching them, and then encouraging me to hire them.

You might have a Renee too – someone who gets (and cares about) your business and is pretty well connected in your sector.

Anyway, I shared that role with Renee and she suggested someone we both knew. Someone who I felt was completely overqualified to work in my business. Would she really be prepared to do all the doing that needed to be done?

It turned out she would – because she liked our business but also, and more importantly, she'd recently had a baby. And she didn't want to work weekends anymore.

My EVP was a perfect fit for her at this moment in her life. It wouldn't have been two years prior, and it might not be in five years. But it worked out for both of us at that moment.[27]

---

[27] I strongly believe that there is no one more efficient or resilient than a working mum. Seconded only by working dads. They can very quickly get to the heart of what matters when there's a toddler throwing a tantrum, dinner needs to be cooked and the baby's nap window is about to close.

So, once you have a clear idea who you're looking for, ask your network. Be open to people outside your industry. Remember, you're looking for skills and attributes, not experience and qualifications.

One of the unexpected outcomes of our EVP is that it is very attractive to freelancers who want to keep building their own business at the same time. Remember, I always wanted to build a business that provides flexibility, autonomy and financial stability. For freelancers stuck in a feast-or-famine cycle, knowing they have a regular part-time paycheque can be very reassuring.

Some business-starters might see that as a risk, though – what if they only stick around long enough to learn your secret sauce and then run off with your clients? And that's certainly a possibility. Which is why you need a boring-but-ironclad employment agreement that covers non-compete and intellectual property. Plus a bit of trust that you've picked a person who aligns with your values.

There's one more thing you can do to make this whole hiring business simpler. Once you're clear on what you need, ask AI to write the draft role description for you, and all those email responses and follow-ups. Many hiring managers tell me this is a time-saving gamechanger for them.

How much do you need to pay people?

As we've already discussed, pay is just one part of the whole package you'll offer your ideal candidate. But it is a make-or-break part, because no one can pay their rent using birthday leave.

Be realistic about what the market is paying for the sort of person you need and how much you can afford to pay.

Benchmark going rates online, and then plug the number you're comfortable with into your breakeven model. (Don't have a breakeven model? Don't panic, we're going to build one later in this chapter.)

Play with a range of scenarios: what happens to your bottom line if your revenue grows 30% as a result of this hire? What if it doesn't grow at all for the next six months? If you cut their days back, does it work better for you?

Be really transparent about your salary range on your job ad. You don't have time to wade through hundreds of applications from people who are expecting twice that. And they don't want to spend time on the application and interview process only to realise at the last hurdle that money will be a deal-breaker.

If it's part time and you're quoting the full-time equivalent salary in the ad, make that crystal clear. Otherwise, you'll be having an awkward conversation after you've emailed the contract.

Finally, if you meet your dream hire but they need a little more money, be prepared to negotiate over time as well as pay. Some of our best flexibility options have come from this process – such as working a seven-day fortnight instead of eight. An extra day off every second week feels like a bonus for a busy working parent – and the work still seems to miraculously get done.

Who don't you need to hire?

There are roles in any business that don't need to be done in house until you become much, much bigger, such as:

- **Bookkeeper and/or accountant:** Outsource these important tasks to a professional adviser on a retainer or annual-fee basis.

- **HR/Talent Manager:** You don't really need a dedicated person taking care of people and culture until you're at around 50 staff. Again, you can outsource specific tasks like recruitment on an ad hoc basis.
- **Marketing Manager:** If digital marketing, social media management or content production is not your area of expertise, and you depend on it to generate leads, outsource this to a marketing agency.
- **Chief Financial Officer:** If you need help setting up financial systems and governance structures and your accountant isn't up for that challenge, bring someone in on a fractional basis.
- **IT support:** Get systems that are easy to self-manage, and outsource big changes if needed.

It's important to be realistic about this, because you may hire someone who dreams of a career path into these areas – and it just might not happen with your business.

Becoming the best boss you can

Playing soccer with a local club for many years led web designer Jordanne Collins to understand success depends on making sure the right person is in the right position: 'A year ago, I didn't think I would ever hire someone. Then I realised it was too much for just me.'

> 'If I found the right person in the right role, and put the right structure around that, I could still do what I loved.'

She says her big focus right now is on being a good leader in her business: 'When you are managing people, leadership makes or breaks a workplace. When it's small like this, it's everything – and it also creates your clients' experience.'

Growing any business requires talent, clients and processes. In my experience, if you get the talent right, the rest is a lot easier. That's why I've spent the first part of this chapter on finding the right people. We'll go into clients and processes next.

But before we do, it's also worth noting that the real work as a boss starts once you get someone on board. Your role as a coach, mentor, manager and leader begins.

My first attempt at managing others in my mid-20s wasn't a roaring success. Second time around, when I decided to build a team at Writers, I was a working mum. I was used to setting expectations with toddlers and making sure they felt cared for.

Looking back, I can see how that influenced my approach to managing others. When I heard how author Liz Wiseman describes negative leadership traits in a workshop, I realised I was a 'rescuer'.[28] I was the one who could be relied on to step in and fix problems.

Turns out, that can 'accidently diminish' the potential of others to find better solutions. People started coming to me with problems rather than ideas. My to-do list kept growing, along with my sense of frustration. And it was frustrating for them too – they didn't feel like clients valued them as much as me, or that they had opportunities to step outside their comfort zone and learn.

Because I was in their way.

---

28   *Multipliers: How the best leaders make everyone smarter*, Greg McKeown & Liz Wiseman, 2017.

Over time, I've learned to trust in my team. Rather than making things easier for them, I have to let them figure out the solution, make mistakes and learn along the way.

Wiseman says 'multiplier' leaders make space for thinking and expect great work. They stretch and challenge their team, and create a sense of ownership and accountability. Sometimes, that's as simple as asking more questions rather than rushing to provide an answer.

The principles of being a great coach include the following:

- **Active listening:** reframe their statements or questions to show you've understood.
- **Pause:** uncomfortable silence shows you they're thinking (resist the urge to jump in with an answer).
- **Look for opportunities to affirm their strengths early in a conversation:** what lights them up when they talk about it? Where does their energy come from? Label it.
- **Ask focused, open questions:** like, 'What have you tried? What else can you do? What change do you expect? What are you assuming about the situation?'

Now you're ready to be the boss. But where will all the extra work come from to keep this thriving team busy? That's what we'll explore next – along with the systems and processes you need in place to feel in control.

LET'S GROW

1. Think about the best boss you've ever had. What did they do differently?

   ....
   ....
   ....
   ....
   ....
   ....
   ....
   ....

2. If you could only hire one role in your business, what would it be? What traits, skills and values would the ideal candidate have?

   ....
   ....
   ....
   ....
   ....
   ....
   ....
   ....

How to stretch your capacity and stay in control

Hiring the right people is only one 'P' in our good growth model, and just one part of running an agency-style business. Without the right structures in place before their first day, you could spiral out of control. Fast.

When I chat with agency founders about what good growth feels like, our answers are a little different to our freelancing friends. That's because people play such a significant role in our growth story.

'I think good business growth would feel like a really consistent cadence of new inquiries, coupled with high team morale and good spirit, plus positive client feedback and the space to explore new things,' says Sarah Spence of her growth utopia.

Janine Pares says good growth means good staff retention for her strategic marketing consultancy. 'A service-based business lives or dies by its people. You need systems and processes so when you add new projects, services or people to the mix, the wheels don't fall off,' she says.

'You also have to trust that things will keep happening the way they should when you're not in the room.'

Carolyn Loton has spent many years building her thriving marketing agency, Juntos Marketing. But as a former occupational therapist turned fast-moving consumer goods marketer, she admits she had no idea how an agency worked when she first set up her own company.

'The smartest thing I could have done was work in another agency for a year. I felt like I had to invent everything – structure, pricing, profitability, what makes a good client and how you go get them,' she says.

You probably don't have time to go work in an agency for a year. And even if you did, you might also pick up some bad habits.

Let's take a look at how you build an agency around the other four Ps: purpose, processes, proposition and profit. Because as well as good people, every thriving agency has these four ingredients:

- **Clear purpose:** everyone understands what they are working towards and what behaviours are expected.
- **Time-saving systems and processes:** the technology, processes and workflow management that make it easier to share the work, and get it done efficiently and to a consistent standard.
- **A strong proposition that draws a steady pipeline of customers:** relationship management systems and expectations, marketing and lead management.
- **Financial stability:** predictable cashflow, consistent pricing, and regular reporting to keep everyone accountable.

Don't wait to build these things *after* you grow. Start with a stable base, even though elements will keep evolving. Ed Gandia tells told me, unless you have the right fee structures, efficient processes and recurring, predictable work in place, 'you'll just magnify the existing problems if you scale before solving them'.

Jess White, CEO and Partner of advertising and PR agency Cassette, has taken her business from a team of eight to over fifty. For her, 'measured and paced growth is absolutely essential'.

'It is no longer enough to be really great at your craft, or to just work really hard. You have to be so much more strategic around how you actually grow a business, and make sure you're growing with a mindset around risk as well as growth.'

By this, she means building a stable business model. It might not sound sexy, but it's how she sleeps at night.

'Every time I walk into the office, I am reminded that the wages and livelihoods of 55 people are on my shoulders,' she says. 'Their next paycheque is on me. I've chosen to build a business, and that's a responsibility. So, a measure of success for me is a stable business that ensures that I am providing appropriately for my team.'

Purpose and values

Clarity of purpose is another measure of success for Jess. Her whole team needs to be able to explain what they're trying to achieve in the next three to five years – not just what they're solving for a client that day.

As I mentioned in chapter 4, it took me 10 years to land on a clearly defined company purpose statement. But from day one, I knew Writers stood for quality over quantity, and for building positive and enduring relationships. That helped me attract the right talent and clients early on.

So, don't panic if your purpose statement isn't quite resonating yet. Just set yourself some boundaries – what is the type of work we do and don't do, and why – and be clear on the values you're hiring for. The rest will evolve over time.

Processes and profit

Growing an agency business is a supply-and-demand juggling act, solving the tension between capacity (available hours) and client conversion (available work). If you think the freelancing feast-or-famine cycle is stressful, keeping three or more creatives busy every day takes that to another level.

To manage the client-capacity tension well – without feeling overwhelmed or under budget – you need systems.

An agency the size of Cassette needs a significant tech stack, which has involved three major IT transformation projects in Jess's 14 years with the agency.

'You can't underestimate the importance of investing in operations and back of house before you grow. If you don't, it will feel too hard, and it will cost you more,' Jess explains.

'If you don't have the right systems and support structures for your people, they're probably going to be operating at 70%. You need them to operate at 100%. I can now see my team doing their best work, with the least pressure and in the most efficient way.'

In an agency business model, processes and profit go hand in hand. To keep earning more than you spend, everyone needs to be working fairly consistently. But reality rarely works that way. Some people will be working flat out on big projects, while others are in limbo, waiting for that promised big brief to land.

Measure the things that matter, and make that visible to everyone. We all need to be conscious of what needs to be done to achieve our shared goals. And we all need to be aware of who needs a break – and who can step in to help carry the load.

Setting yourself up for success

So, let's get all nerdy and dig into how you can set yourself up to do that.

Financial stability

If you're serious about building a business you feel in control of, you need to get financial systems in place.

When your business is fairly simple, it's probably enough to keep an eye on revenue fluctuations and make sure you're earning more than you spend over any given year. But making the choice to be bigger than yourself means taking responsibility for your financial stability. That means setting some targets and keeping an eye on the numbers that matter most.

Of course, if you spend too much time nitpicking numbers to feel in financial control or re-entering data across lots of different systems, you'll have less time for the actual revenue-making work. Your financial systems should be idiot-proof in their ease of use and 100% accurate. An accounting platform is essential – aim to make invoicing, analysis, tax and payroll all simple, 10-minute tasks. To avoid the error-prone effort of having to re-enter client, quote and job details, make sure it includes or syncs up with a workflow management tool.

Some accounting platforms have add-on apps for cashflow modelling, turbocharged business intelligence or customer relationship management.

If spreadsheets aren't your natural habitat, ask your accountant to help you set up some basic reporting – and ask plenty of questions to make sure you understand what the reports mean.

These numbers are the key to understanding the consequences of every decision you make.[29]

When it comes to making business decisions with financial implications (which is pretty much any decision), there is one tool I turn to: a breakeven model. Basically, it's a spreadsheet that lets me play with different scenarios.

Here are the raw ingredients for an agency breakeven model.

1. Start with the talent

List all the billable in-house people you employ (even if that's just you), their annual salary and total employable hours per year. By billable, I mean people who do the work you can charge clients directly for: designers, writers, coders, strategists.

Work out their on-costs as a percentage; for example, if you offer 25 days paid annual leave, that's 200 hours. If a full-time role is 1976 hours, annual leave adds 10.1% to your salary costs (200 ÷ 1976). Any other regulated employment costs in your country – including paid public holidays, sick leave, superannuation and workers compensation insurance – should be included here.

Calculate their hourly rate based on the payroll plus on-costs. (Lightbulb moment: are you charging your clients enough?)

Now list all the non-billable people you employ and their annual salary. That's your account manager, project coordinator, marketing assistant or admin. Add in their on-costs. You don't need an hourly rate for them, as they're not billable (but if you now realise they should be, this helps you work out how to charge for their time).

---

29 If you want to build a business with saleable value one day, robust financial systems are mission critical, and the more historical reporting you can draw on, the better. One day, you'll have to lift the lid on all your systems and financial structures, and you'll need accurate analysis and projections at your fingertips.

These two lines together, with the on-costs, are your total payroll overheads.

2. Next, mix in your expenses

Separate expenses by fixed and variable costs, and write the annual cost next to each.

Fixed overheads are things you can't really negotiate once they're locked in:

- accounting fees
- software and cloud services subscriptions
- bank charges
- legal fees
- insurance
- office expenses
- phone
- staff training and development
- rent
- electricity.

Variable costs can be increased or decreased, depending how things are going:

- travel
- entertainment
- business development
- advertising
- website
- ad hoc freelancers or contractors.

3. Add it all up

Add your payroll overheads and total expenses together to get your annual breakeven. Ouch. Divide it by 12 to get your monthly breakeven. That's the minimum amount you need to invoice every month just to stay afloat.

4. Check your capacity

Is it even realistic to invoice that much each month? Check the number of total hours you have available from your billable talent.

Here's an example. Let's say you work full time in your business and you're the only billable employee. Your average charge rate is $150. If you are only charging for time, your business revenue target cannot realistically exceed $296,400 – and that's working solely on client projects, 38 hours a week, 52 weeks a year.

When you have a mix of part-time and full-time staff, it can be hard to keep tabs on how much capacity you have. This spreadsheet can help you see it.

Of course, no one is going to work flat out every day of the year. And not all your time is billable anyway. Apply a rule to your hourly rate – maybe you feel 70% of your time is billable. Then take out your annual leave.

Now how much revenue can you realistically target?

Once you are clear on these numbers, you can see how important efficiency is. You can charge the equivalent of 10 hours for a project, and if you nail it in six, you're starting to build a buffer in your profit margin.

And that's what you should be aiming for – because it allows you to stretch your revenue beyond the number of hours you want to work. It also gives you a safety net for unexpected expenses.

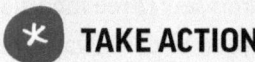 **TAKE ACTION**

I've created a basic breakeven model spreadsheet that you can adapt for your business. Don't forget to check your calculations with your accountant!

Download your breakeven model at **beyondsolo.co**.

Do you really need an annual budget? The short answer is *yes*. However, no one is going to fire you for not meeting key performance indicators (KPIs) in your own business. Think of it as a 'loose' goal, a baseline to plan around.

Most freelancers I've spoken to told me they don't set a budget. I get it – it's not much fun. Maybe unrealistic targets are why you kicked a corporate job to the kerb.

Jordanne says she struggled with the pressure of working towards a stretch target. 'I know how much I have to make each month; I've got my minimum,' she explains. 'But when I set a higher yearly goal, it took the fun out of it all. I love every aspect of running my business. I think everyone needs to figure out how they're best driven – for me, the pressure brought me down.'

Similarly, Oyelola found that setting targets made her focus too much on the financials when her main goal at this time is to build a business she finds fulfilling.

But here's the thing:

> When you keep yourself accountable to a budget for income, expenses and profit, you stay focused on bringing in and turning around consistent work.

That's why freelance writer Amy Ragland sets three income targets for herself at the start of every year. She is always striving towards a stretch goal, but she knows what her minimum needs to be.

When you have a breakeven model and a budget, you can quickly check the impact of every great idea before you commit:

- If you hire a creative sidekick, what will that do to cashflow?
- Can you afford to pay their salary if it takes six months for revenue growth to kick in?
- What is the likely revenue uptick based on the capacity they add or free up?
- If you give everyone more annual leave as part of your wellbeing policy, what happens to your billable capacity?
- When someone asks you for a (well-deserved) pay bump, what might it mean for your profit?

So, is there any science to coming up with a revenue target? Here are a few options:

- Add up all the costs of doing business from your breakeven, plus your target profit number. That's the revenue you need to earn. Simple.
- Look at your last three or four years of revenue. What's your average growth percentage? Stretch that a little – maybe just enough that it feels challenging but real – and add it to last year's income.
- Target the average growth benchmarks in your industry. For a creative agency, according to a few successful owners I've spoken with, that number is 20% to 30%. Add that to last year's income.

This last one was a bit of a wake-up call for me. When creative agency founder Sue-Ella McDowall told me she benchmarked

25% year-on-year growth for 25 years (the only time they missed that was during the Global Financial Crisis), I felt guilty about my own periods of utter flatlining.

But let's remember, we're working towards *good* business growth – and what that means to you may be different to what it means to others.

Brand agency founder Peter Fuller says he also used 20% to 30% revenue growth as a base benchmark of success – but over the many decades he's been operating, it could be 100% growth one year and 10% the next. He says:

'If you're aiming for no-growth because you don't want the hassles that come with size, you're likely going backwards given cost increases and market fluctuations.'

'Twenty per cent is steady, manageable growth that safeguards against natural attrition of clients. However, there is no point growing for the sake of growth, or to meet the expectations of other people,' he says.

Time-saving systems and processes

One of the best tech decisions I made was using a workflow management system early in my freelancing life. I was already struggling to keep track of all the deadlines, project scope and invoices, and it immediately saved me time by almost automating quotes, job data and invoicing.

So if you don't already have something that does that, now is the time.

Now is the time to also start tracking your time. Seriously, this is non-negotiable.

Whether you charge by the project, by the hour, or for value, you're still basically selling your time. If you don't know where you're spending that finite resource, you're on a fast track to profitless prosperity – that's where money is coming in the door but there's nothing left for you.

As several seasoned agency owners told me, if you're not making a profit, you're ultimately going broke. So make sure your systems make it easy to track the data that matters to you.

For me, that means things like:

- time on billable vs non-billable work
- profit (based on our hourly costs including overheads) per project, sector and job category
- top 10 clients by contribution to revenue.

Your metrics might be different. For example, you might need to keep a closer eye on quote conversion, or the value of projects in your pipeline. Work out what drives your business growth and profitability, and then measure and track it.

Must-have systems and processes

What do you really need to keep your business humming along? This will depend on the type of work you do – if you're a marketing consultant, SEO or social media tools might be business-critical. If you're a copywriter, you might find AI-enabled transcription and generative AI tools are a gamechanger.

Most consultants and freelancers growing beyond solo will need to tick off these eight essentials.

1. **Workflow management:** track all your projects from lead to quote to scope to invoice, time-keeping, client information and reporting.
2. **Accounting:** financial records, reconciliation, expenses, profit and loss, balance sheet, cashflow and breakeven analysis.
3. **Communication channels:** emails, Slack-style channels for urgent conversations, video meeting platforms.
4. **Central file storage or drive:** so you all have remote access to real-time versions.
5. **Client relationship management (CRM) platform and marketing tools:** client database, email and lead nurture campaigns, design platforms.
6. **People management:** employment contracts, job roles, performance and development frameworks, wellbeing and working-from-home policies.
7. **Client management:** terms of work, non-disclosure agreements.
8. **Templates and checklists:** briefs, proposals, presentations, client and employee welcome packs, invoices, email footers – any documents you use regularly can and should be templated.

With all the different business management tools available, it can be very easy to blow your budget on monthly subscriptions. It's surprising how quickly $10 per user per month adds up when you have an ever-growing number of software systems. Clients also generally expect you to be system-agnostic so you can collaborate with them, which may also involve multiple platforms.

Before you sign up for the latest must-have tech platform, think about the problems you really need to solve. You may find there is a better (possibly free) solution.

Get into a workflow rhythm

Whether you're working with one other person or several, set regular check-ins to make sure you're all working towards the same objectives. This might mean a weekly work-in-progress (WIP) meeting or daily five-minute 'stand-ups'.

And now you're the boss, it's time to make time for regular one-on-one check-ins. Everyone wants to feel their voice is heard, their ideas are valued and they have opportunities to continually improve. That might be a quick coffee chat about how things are going, or more formal development reviews.

I've learned the hard way how important it is to provide feedback in the moment. I don't love delivering bad news (who does?), but if I let things slide it will come back to bite me, them and the business as a missed learning opportunity and (probably) a pissed-off client. So, don't leave that to the end of the financial year. And be prepared to receive feedback from your team with good grace as well.

Propositions and pipeline

I could spend an entire book on strategies to win – and keep – more clients. And of course, your creative agency won't grow without them. If you're now wondering how you're going to keep your staff consistently busy, here are five levers you can pull. See what works for you.

Get clear on your client value proposition

In chapter 5, we talked at length about creating an employee value proposition (EVP). Let's go back to what that means for your clients.

What do you do that no one else does? How does that add value for your clients?

If you're not sure, ask them. The answers may surprise you. Clients rarely make rational decisions based on experience, track record, expertise in their sector or business, or price. The truth is more emotional. We all want to work with people who are easy to work with. We enjoy working with people who bring energy and enthusiasm, who don't just treat us like one of a hundred clients.

Talk to a few different clients, and look for patterns in their responses. Then go back to your purpose and values. Hopefully, the way clients want to work with you aligns with how you like to work and what you stand for.

Now, make sure this message is clear on your website, proposal templates, social media pages – everything you share externally. Don't be afraid to use the words your clients give you, as they make your marketing genuine and relatable.

Once you know the true value of the value you bring, the pricing conversation also gets easier.

When you're scoping out a brief, ask the client to describe the underlying problem they need to solve and how they'll measure a good outcome. You could then ask them what budget they think is reasonable to achieve that.

If they come back with a lowball price, that's a red flag. Explain they won't get what they're hoping for at that price.

Get your pricing just right and you'll build trust in your core value proposition.

Build enduring relationships

My mantra for persuasive copywriting is 'solve, don't sell'. It's the same for business development. No one wants to be interrupted by a sales pitch. However, everyone has problems they need help with.

To understand what those problems are, and how your services can help, you need to invest a little time in one-on-one conversations. That's the only way to become the holy grail of professional consultants: a trusted adviser.

And it's the key to building enduring relationships.

People do business with people. Not with brands or business entities. Those people will go on to work for other businesses in their long careers, and if they have a positive working relationship with you, they'll take you with them.

As a solo graphic designer in the late 1980s, Sue-Ella McDowall landed several major clients within her first few years – including Lendlease. Every opportunity started with a warm introduction and a coffee. All of them led to ongoing work. And within a decade, she'd built the go-to marketing agency for the property industry.

Don't underestimate the value of being personable. And make time for in-real-life coffee catch-ups.

Aim for recurring work

Repeat business is essential for good growth. You'll spend less time chasing new clients, and (in most cases) you'll get more efficient at the work you do because you know those clients and their businesses so well.

This is easier for some services than others. Many managers need regular support from designers or content creators. But they'll only build a new website or implement a transformation strategy once or twice in a decade.

If your specialty tends towards the one-off projects, think about how you can extend that into recurring work. Think brand consultancy plus sales enablement tools. Or, web builds plus search optimisation and social media management.

When I first started my agency, I believed retainers were a lose-lose proposition. I'd end up doing way more work than the retainer allowed, with my income capped – or my client wouldn't see anything much happening and start resenting that monthly payment. It felt like a fixed project fee was more transparent for both sides.

However, a fixed project fee puts all the risk on you as the supplier. If you don't set clear scope expectations upfront, that's on you. If the job takes longer, that's also on you. And if it gets put on hold, there's often only so much you can charge – unless you have a delay fee.

In contrast, regular and predictable revenue – which a retainer can provide – is a sanity-saver for cashflow. It means you don't need to spend as much time hustling your project pipeline. And it's a foundation of business value for any future investor or partner.

For example, my accountant charges me monthly for a bundle of services: wrapping up end-of-year company statements, quarterly reporting, monthly tax compliance and payroll, and ad hoc financial issues. All in one easy-on-my-cashflow fee. I sign an agreement at the beginning of each financial year. Everything is clear and predictable for both parties.

When accounting firms like this are valued by a third party – for a bank loan, or by another firm looking to acquire or merge – the value of their client book matters. And that's the value of that locked-in, recurring revenue.

Think about your own regular clients. Can you put a value on that 'book' of maintainable revenue?

If you want to experiment with retainer pricing, try redefining a retainer as a 'subscription model' – which it effectively is. That could be a strategy subscription or a repeat engagement as a fractional consultant. If that works, you could set yourself up to productise some of the recurring services by defining processes, automating what you can and outsourcing other tasks.

Nothing is forever, of course. There's nothing to stop me from switching accountants.

Retainer contracts can be cancelled. You might get sick of turning over the same work. You still need a new business pipeline. But if you want to build tangible value into your business because you hope one day to sell it, lock in that recurring revenue where you can.

Ask for referrals

What if your client's happiness could unlock the easiest route to marketing? Nielsen's global Trust in Advertising study found

88% of customers trust recommendations from people they know above all other forms of marketing messaging.[30]

As a consultant or freelancer, you are essentially in the business of helping people: solving their problems, taking things off their to-do list, making them look good in front of their boss or the board. If you do that really well, those clients will become your best advocates – and a valuable unpaid sales team.

The fastest and easiest way to win new clients is through a warm (or, even better, glowing) referral. They'll already trust you to get the work done and are less likely to push back on pricing or timing.

When you're doing good work, referrals should happen naturally. However, some clients may be reluctant to share you for fear of losing your time and attention. That's why you may need to set up a more conscious referral strategy. Here are five steps to take.

1. **Make referral requests obvious.** Add a line to your email footer and invoice template so that request is always top of mind for your clients.
2. **Look for opportunities to build your network within a big organisation.** Ask for a warm introduction to other teams or parts of the business that could use your services.
3. **Thank people who refer you.** Yes, that seems obvious. But it's easy to forget. Send a thoughtful gift to your strongest allies – the surprise and delight factor goes a long way to keeping that relationship strong.
4. **Make sure you deliver on your next promise.** There's nothing worse than referring someone and discovering

---

30 Nielsen Trust in Advertising, 2021, https://www.nielsen.com/wp-content/uploads/sites/2/2021/11/2021-Nielsen-Trust-In-Advertising-Sell-Sheet.pdf.

later they let you down. You'll be very unlikely to refer them again.
5. **Add social proof to your proposals.** Ask for testimonials, and use them widely: on your website, on case studies, in proposals and quotes, and on social media.

Be consistent with marketing

How often should you be marketing your agency?

Every single day.

That's how you stay visible. Getting more work is a matter of being seen in the right place at the right time. Web designer Jordanne Collins tells me she worked out just 2% of her audience sees a social post at any point in time.

'I would send one email or write one post, and then not do anything for three months because I got busy. And then things got quiet. I realised I had to talk consistently about my business,' she says.

Jordanne acknowledges the 'high highs and low lows' of demand took her by surprise in the first few years of her business. 'It was almost self-sabotaging. I didn't want to be overwhelmed by more work, so I'd retreat into my cocoon to do what was in front of me. And then I'd emerge, realising I needed the next thing.'

That's why she took on her first staff member. It helped her be more consistent and make marketing a daily habit.

For you, that habit might mean just 10 minutes a day on any of these activities:

- posting on social media
- writing a lead nurture email journey for web subscribers

- planning an email to your database
- writing a blog or ebook
- planning a webinar or event.

Emails to your mailing list are probably the most underrated tool for small business growth. They are an opportunity to share your knowledge, build trust and show your value. And it takes the same time to reach one person as 10,000 if you have some simple systems in place.

However, not all emails are good emails. If you want your email to result in more work, rather than an immediate delete or (worse) unsubscribe, you need to put a bit of thought into what you say.

Plan your email marketing around these three principles:

- **What's in it for them?** Make sure your email earns its place in your reader's inbox by being relevant, timely and useful. How can you solve a problem they're dealing with, share some practical tips or make them smile?
- **What works best?** Test your email send days, times, subject lines and calls to action. Try segmenting your database; for example, you could tailor industry-relevant tips to one audience group. Track your results against industry benchmarks.
- **What do you want to achieve?** Read your email once more before you schedule it. Is your main message crystal clear? Don't expect your reader to catch 10 different ideas in one paragraph – start and end your email with what you want them to know, think or do.

Staying top of mind is a numbers game. Your goal is to remind prospects and clients you exist at the exact moment they realise they need your help. You can only do that if you are consistent with email marketing, social posts and web content.

Keep following up

With these five tactics in place, you should start generating more consistent leads. Which means you need a system to track and manage that pipeline. Your workflow management tool might give you a way to capture and visualise leads before they turn into a quote, or you may find another tool works best for you. Record as much information as you can upfront, including the project scope, potential value, timeframe and referral source, to streamline the conversion process later.

Then, make someone responsible for following up or nudging busy clients. They'll appreciate you reminding them about that great idea they had in the last meeting, and they're more likely to ask you for help with the next step.

From people to profit models, we've covered all the essential elements of starting and growing a traditional agency model. And many of these principles and strategies will apply to other models as well.

And what if you don't want the burden of payroll, or the responsibility of managing others? If this chapter convinced you an agency isn't your vibe, fear not. There is another way to work with other talented people – as part of a collective. We'll explore what that takes in the next chapter.

# ARE YOU READY TO RUN A SMALL BUSINESS?

The small business path might be right for you if:

- ✓ you want to be the boss – spending more time managing or coaching others, less time doing the billable work
- ✓ you have three to six months of operating expenses in your business bank account – including your salary
- ✓ you know the difference you make to your clients, what sets you apart, and your purpose and values
- ✓ you have systems and processes for tracking time, measuring profit and managing payroll.

The small business path might *not* be right for you if:

- ✗ you don't want the financial pressure of making payroll every month.

LET'S GROW

Before we explore some alternative paths to growth, make a few notes to identify gaps and opportunities in your current systems and processes.

1. Download the Agency Breakeven Model at beyondsolo.co and start plugging in your numbers. Are your revenue targets realistic? What is the impact if you add a staff member? Play with some scenarios, and make a few notes.

2. What systems do you have in place now? What do you need? Check them off here.

Have Need

Have	Need	
☐	☐	Workflow management platform
☐	☐	Accounting platform
☐	☐	Communication channels
☐	☐	Video call platform
☐	☐	Central file storage or drive
☐	☐	Client relationship management (CRM) platform
☐	☐	Employee and client contracts and policies
☐	☐	Workflow templates and checklists
☐	☐	Other: _____
☐	☐	Other: _____
☐	☐	Other: _____

Let's disrupt the traditional agency model by bringing together the best of the best talent as a collective or cooperative.

8: Beyond solo to collective: A-Team collaboration

Tapping into the expertise of likeminded freelancers

If you grew up in the 1980s like me, you might remember a show called *The A-Team*. Four former commandos worked together to take on various missions, each with their own skills and personality.

Think low-fi version of The Avengers. Six Hulks working together might not get to the heart of the challenge and save the world – but when Hulk gets together with Iron Man and the gang, there's nothing they can't do. It's a collective model that draws together diverse strengths to create a united superpower.

The A-Team Collective is a type of outsourcing model with a fundamental difference: it's not dependent on you alone to land or manage a client project.

It's a shared responsibility.

One person might take the lead on any given job, but that decision will vary depending on the scope's focus. You all bring relatively similar levels of experience, but across complementary skillsets, so if the project is technical (like a web rebuild), the technical expert is more likely to run the project. If it's more strategic, the change consultant might be in charge.

Done well – whether it's an ad hoc cooperative or structured collective – this model has the potential to disrupt the traditional agency market. Clients want to work with the best professionals, not the junior intern. This model gives them a whole tribe of trusted experts to solve their problems, with one point of contact for project management and invoicing.

With increased budget scrutiny, many clients are becoming less willing to pay agency admin-style account service fees – and that has slowly been eroding the traditional agency margin structure.

These reasons contribute to design agency founder Sue-Ella McDowall's belief that the collective model is the future.

'If I ever started another agency, I would do it differently. I would bring in more expert partners and form a collective,' she says.

Sue-Ella and I worked together as a collective recently, and the experience was – in Sue-Ella's words – 'the ultimate'.

'It worked. It was a huge success as a campaign, everyone was paid their worth, and we cut through all the layers of decision-making,' she says.

The different collective models

Collective models can be loose or structured. You can come together for a single project, tapping the best possible individuals for each aspect of that job, and then disband. That's a loose model. Or you can have a structured collective, where you are part of an ongoing ecosystem of freelance talent, and everyone shares in the communal success. This might look and feel like a traditional agency, but potentially without the payroll burden.

From the client's perspective, a collective also feels like a traditional agency, but without a gatekeeper between them and their consultant. This is what removes unnecessary layers of admin and communication – and the risks of misunderstanding the brief, or wasting time and resources.

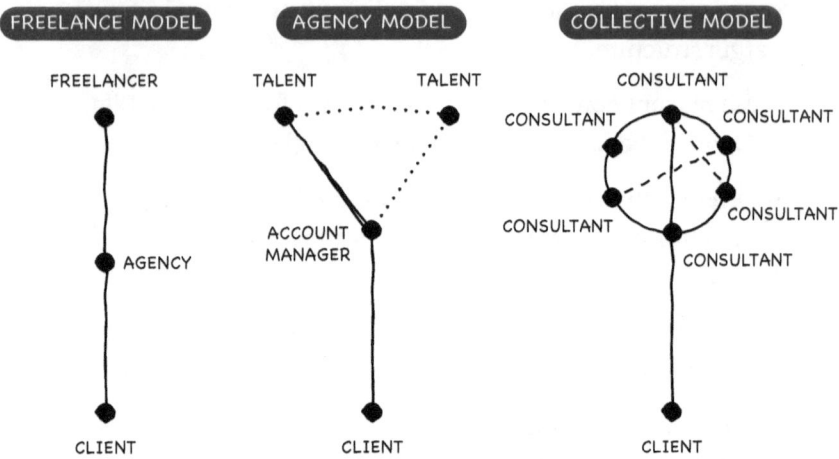

Loose collective: flex around the work

One person in a collective needs to take responsibility for managing each project – keeping track of timelines, budgets and client expectations. That one point of contact also makes things easier for the client.

Budgets are transparent and shared fairly according to the work required. In my experience, copywriting rarely gets allocated as much budget as design, but when Sue-Ella and I worked on that campaign as a collective, it was a narrative-led strategy. That demanded more writing time and thinking from me – which meant I received a fairer share of the budget than if I'd been freelancing for an agency.

A strong collective shares the essential attributes of any high-performing team.

There needs to be trust and respect between members of a collective. Understand the different roles you play and how you can make the most of individual strengths while feeling safe to challenge ideas.

In other words, no egos.

In the case of our collective project, the client had nothing but good things to say about her experience and the outcome.

'It was the best decision ever,' she told me. 'The traditional agency model has more overheads, more people involved, more process and red tape, and certainly more cost.'[31]

'Having independent experts, leaders at what they do, really appealed,' she added. 'By removing the middle person, I could build a closer relationship with each of those people. I'm dealing directly with the person who's making the decisions and is responsible for the output. Turnaround times are faster. We cut out a lot of unnecessary communication. And I think it's more flexible.'

So clients love this model. And we had a great experience working with each other.

Where's the downside? Imagine we all formed a commune where we can share equally in the fruits of our labour, but we don't have a formal agreement on who buys the tractor and seeds, and who is responsible for planting and harvesting. That can be the problem with a loose collective.

---

[31] This is also worth noting if you're planning on growing a traditional agency. Consciously avoiding some of these things could be your competitive advantage.

> It's harder to sustain your collective's business development momentum if no one is technically responsible for that on a day-to-day basis.

But it's a business model UK-based copywriter Jo Marshall believes is worth exploring. She's recently formed an alliance with a local brand agency, web development business, research agency and video content agency who – like her – all focus on higher education clients.

'After working together on a few university projects, we realised we were all doing good work that together solved different parts of the communication puzzle for universities – a process that is often disconnected,' Jo explains. 'The client might engage someone to do the brand, but that strategy and messaging doesn't always filter into the essential elements of execution, and the result is a watered-down brand and comms.'

The group decided to create a better experience for everyone by joining forces and targeting bigger projects together.

'It's already led to larger scale projects than any of us would have usually gone after on our own,' Jo says.

In their early conversations, the group agreed one person or agency would take the lead on client management, depending on the primary scope of the brief. That person would then subcontract to the others.

'A client doesn't want to have to deal with five different agencies, so it solves that problem for them,' says Jo. Her collective model also has an advantage with its very narrow university focus – the group is more likely to get new business through referrals and one-on-one conversations over coffee and by sharing case studies that showcase their individual and combined impact in that sector.

However, they also need to challenge the status quo of how creative work gets done: their clients are used to working with a traditional agency with the perceived stability of an in-house team and a balance sheet. They need to show how their approach will reduce project risk rather than create it.

And once they do land the work, they need to avoid the perennial issue with any group project: one person could end up carrying the load, get frustrated and drop out.

But so far, Jo says, the collective model is showing promising signs in terms of offering a new and more effective result for the higher education sector.

It's certainly true that collaborating with your peers in a loose collective model can give you fresh ideas and push you to stretch and develop your own capabilities. It's also refreshing to share the burden of problem-solving with awesome people in related fields. You can take on larger or more complex contracts with bigger budgets.

In theory, this model also frees up a load of admin time with zero HR obligations and lower overheads.

But landing big jobs as a loose collective can be challenging – especially if everyone in the group is too busy with their own work to take the lead on chasing referrals or submitting tenders. A more formal structure with clear expectations might help you unlock the full potential of a loose collective.

Here are a few things to consider:

- Who's responsible for finding and converting leads?
- Do you compensate that person for the time it takes to prospect leads? (For example, a commission once the invoice is paid.)
- How will you divvy up the budget?
- Who's best placed to make sure the project is delivered on time? (This might be the person with the best eye for detail, rather than the person who has the core skillset.)
- Who's the best person to take responsibility for quality control?

Consultancy cooperatives: for the benefit of all

Cooperative models are one way to build a little more structure into a collective approach. Co-ops have been around since the Industrial Revolution, and you may be familiar with them as mutual societies, agricultural produce distributors or community clubs.

A cooperative can be defined as a member-owned business structure with a minimum number of members (in Australia, that minimum is five). Every member has an equal say, and the cooperative can distribute profits equally to members.

For knowledge workers, banding together as a cooperative could be one way to collaborate within a shared ownership structure. Work comes in via the co-op's brand, and teams are formed around the work. The co-op manages all the shared services, such as insurance, finance, marketing, tech platforms and compliance. This is potentially more cost-effective than doing it all on your own as an individual consultant.

It feels like a partnership model with a social enterprise sense of purpose. Or perhaps it's more like a knowledge worker version of Chinese consumer electronics company Haier's decentralised model, which operates as a network of hundreds of tiny enterprises run by a few employee-entrepreneurs (or 'intrapreneurs').[32] Each is responsible for profitability and customer satisfaction, and can tap into the support services it needs with complete autonomy.

If you feel strongly about creating a business with a social purpose, a co-op could be an interesting model to explore. Co-ops look beyond making a profit to consider *how* they make it, and what they do with that profit to bring value to their members and community.

UK research suggests co-ops are also more likely to survive their first five years compared with other small businesses, although they make up less than 1% of the economy.[33]

It's possible that cooperatives, where a group of members are willing to patiently build up capital, are more resilient than short-term-focused business founders who might be chasing growth for growth's sake. It's also interesting to note the UK already has around 300 co-ops in the digital, professional and legal services sectors – collectively they generated over £115 million revenue in 2023.[34]

If you're excited by the possibility of an employee-owned business, a cooperative isn't the only way. We'll explore

---

32 'Is Organizational Hierarchy Getting in the Way of Innovation?', Kaihan Krippendorff and Claudio Garcia, *Harvard Business Review*, September 2023.
33 Co-operatives UK: uk.coop/understanding-co-ops/what-co-op.
34 'Co-Operative and Mutual Economy 2023', Co-Operatives UK: uk.coop/resources/co-operative-and-mutual-economy-2023.

employee equity options in chapter 11, when we look at exit strategies.

Structured collective: company without constraints

US-based content marketing agency Optimist looks like a decentralised consulting firm. Everyone works remotely, and there's no management hierarchy.

When he started Optimist in 2016, Tyler Hakes had a utopian vision for a new type of agency structure that combined the best elements of freelance work with agency capabilities by giving a collective of experienced freelancers a share of the profits in addition to their rates.

'I had this idealistic notion that I'd get good people, give them some ownership stake, send them on a path, and they'd figure it out and deliver the best work they can. I think that is still possible, but we learned we need a lot of systems to support it,' he says.

Every member of the Optimist team, freelancers and contractors, receives a share of the profits generated each month in addition to fees for their work. The share of profits varies according to seniority, role and workload, so it fluctuates.

Optimist now has around 20 to 25 independent contractors, including one dedicated operations manager. Tyler is the only salaried employee.

Optimist is defining the agency model in a way that works for its clients and its talent. It hasn't always been easy. With a niche focus on content marketing for product-led software companies, revenue took a hit when US start-ups struggled with venture capital funding. But it is inherently flexible, which allows Tyler to adapt to market shifts.

I asked Tyler to unpack how he pulls each of the Five P levers to build his business.

Purpose

'The purpose of Optimist is to put everyone in our team in the best position to do the best possible work,' explains Tyler. With a dispersed team, everyone needs to be aligned to common values – that's what guides every decision and action. These include *doing what's right* and *asking why*. The culture is defined by autonomy – which is a constant balancing act for Tyler.

'My guiding ethos is that if I put the right person in the right seat, give them the right context, give them the right amount of autonomy, ultimately that will lead to the best possible outcome for us and our clients,' he says. 'I am just tweaking those dials all the time to find the right level.'

Proposition

Tyler wanted to combine the best elements of an agency and of working as a freelancer in Optimist. Having worked in agencies for many years, he knew how frustrating the layers of bureaucracy are for staff – and clients.

'The account manager would talk to the client, and then they'd talk to the strategist, and they'd talk to the copywriter. It was so much back and forth. That's why I wanted Optimist to be super flat. I was looking for a way to avoid the traditional hierarchy but still do really great work for clients.'

That's a compelling proposition for clients:

> 'Because we're so flat, we don't have a B-Team. Clients feel they have direct access to the best talent – they aren't being sold by one person and then handed off to the folks behind the scenes.'

'Technically, we have an infinite pool of talent. If a client wants an expert on social media management software on their project, there's a good chance we can customise a team to suit,' he adds.

People

Tyler says the only stakeholders in his business are his team and his clients. So how does he find and keep them?

First, the talent. Optimist pays decent rates plus the profit share. In terms of other benefits, there might be an annual in-real-life retreat and some banter on Slack, but that's pretty much it – freelancers can't come in expecting structured coaching and career path development.

That arrangement attracts a certain type of freelancer – one who wants to be part of building something, who also wants autonomy and space, and who doesn't need a lot of hand-holding.

> 'I think our people feel good about the fractional ownership idea, and that they're contributing to something bigger than themselves.'

Plus, it's flexible. Optimist's freelancers are not on the hook with a fixed share of equity – they can scale their work up and down, and that's what drives their profit share.

As for clients, that's where Tyler has proven his content marketing expertise by building an inbound lead generator: 'It's my job to bring in the work, but 100% of our work comes to us. We get referrals, we have strong relationships in the sector. No one is doing any traditional sales here.'

Processes

Without robust systems and workflow processes, Optimist wouldn't work. Tyler admits he gets really excited about workflows and now has a workflow for continually improving his workflows. Productising his services and deliverables makes it easier to define consistent roles and output, but he says they also need to be able to move quickly and adapt to market changes.

'AI is impacting the traditional content playbook, 1000%,' he acknowledges. 'We need to rethink our packages and solve problems in new ways.'

Profit

So has Tyler's model been successful? Optimist quickly grew to generate over $1 million in revenue, but like many agencies I spoke with it hit a wall – and at one point only posted 7% profit. That's not much to share among the collective.

Tyler credits Mike Michalowicz's book *Profit First* with helping him focus first on a new profit goal and then work backwards to allocate budget. He quickly realised his operating expenses were 77% of revenue – and that wasn't sustainable. One lever he could pull was shifting hourly rates to flat project fees for better control.

Aligning incentives

When you're working with the best of the best, they expect to be paid for their expertise and the value they bring. That's only fair – but it does mean you need to be very careful about how you share the rewards of every project.

With a loose, project-based approach, you have visibility of the client budget and can allocate according to workload or value. Everyone is working towards the same goal on a defined project.

But when you have a more structured collective agency, everyone is working on different things and different projects at any point in time. Tyler's model productises the client package with a flat, predictable fee. That's the output. Working out the input – the freelancer hours and scope – is actually much harder.

Paying an hourly rate makes it easy to assign ad hoc work on the fly. However, the time it takes to do that work can be unpredictable, and that makes it harder to maintain your profit margin. Anyone who does any kind of knowledge work knows the time it takes can be infinite if you don't have boundaries – you can always edit an article one more time, go deeper into a research rabbit hole or come up with one more graphic option. And if you know you'll be paid for every hour that takes, and you have the time, why wouldn't you?

The problem is, Optimist's pricing model offers clients a flat predictable monthly fee. That extra effort isn't in the budget.

Tyler says moving to a flat freelance fee per task encouraged everyone to earn a higher effective hourly rate by finding ways to be more efficient. They still had to maintain the quality, of course. It also made it easier for him to control his biggest cost: contractor fees.

However, it took time to work out exactly the right amount to pay for the different tasks involved in any given piece of work. And that's almost a one-way street: once you set that fee expectation, it's very difficult to change.

The same is true, of course, of your client pricing model. Which is why systems are so critical to making the structured collective work.

Scaling a collective

Ecosystem platforms like Airbnb leverage a network effect for exponential growth. But ecosystem agencies are different. Collective models come with limits.

With very flat structures and little management oversight, rapid growth can quickly turn into exponential chaos. Plus, the more people in the collective, the more that profit share gets diluted.

So it's important to be realistic about your goals if you choose the collective path. Think about the optimal number of freelancers, clients and services you want to manage. Expanding carelessly by trying to be all things to all people will only create headaches.

This is a model where you want to aim for calm, manageable growth: it's far easier to work with fewer clients, and a trusted group of experts.

> **? ARE YOU READY TO CREATE A COLLECTIVE?**
>
> **The ecosystem model might be right for you if:**
>
> - ✓ you have a strong network of experienced freelancers or consultants with specialist skills
> - ✓ your clients want to work with the best talent
> - ✓ you're willing to take on or designate responsibility for lead generation and project management
> - ✓ you don't want management hierarchy
> - ✓ you're willing to share project budget based on contribution.
>
> **The ecosystem model might *not* be right for you if:**
>
> - ✗ you have trust or visibility issues. This model is only as good as the talent and systems – that's the only way to avoid chaos and ensure effective collaboration.

LET'S GROW

If the collective model appeals to you, make a few notes now before you move on.

1. What type of model would work best for you and your clients: loose, cooperative or structured? Why?

   ....

   ....

   ....

   ....

   ....

   ....

   ....

   ....

2. Who do you already have in your future A-Team? What types of specialists are you missing in your network?

   ....

   ....

   ....

   ....

   ....

   ....

   ....

   ....

'Every sale is **an evergreen echo** of something I've built before.'

Lindy Alexander

9: Beyond solo to set-and-forget income: subscriptions and products

Want to make money while you sleep? Here's what that takes

Most of the challenges shared by freelancers and consultants boil down to one thing: trading time for money. Your earning capacity is limited by the number of hours you're prepared to work and how your clients value your efforts. Every client problem and every project is different, and while you can set up processes to automate some of the admin, the actual thinking and doing always seems to take a lot of time.

Passive income flips that narrative: it's income that isn't timebound.

I'm yet to meet a business owner who is experiencing the utopia of guaranteed income. But some are able to generate more revenue without incremental effort. For example, an app can collect subscription income 24 hours a day, seven days a week.

That's the appeal of turning your expertise into a product. A training program, community, toolkit or subscription model that you only need to build once. Then sell over and over again.

Freelancer coach Ed Gandia is a big believer in developing a passive income stream, because it diversifies your revenue sources, which in turn eases a whole lot of business risk.

'Think about this: how would your decisions about what clients or opportunities to accept be different if you had a steady stream of passive income coming in every month?' he says.

In Ed's case, this passive income comes from an online store of business-building toolkit sessions for freelancers, with sample scripts and cheat sheets.

'Having steady revenue outside of my client work coming in the door every month is very reassuring,' he says.

Lindy Alexander describes product revenue as 'evergreen income' rather than passive. 'Every sale is an evergreen echo of something I've built before,' she says. As an online freelance writing coach, she sells resources like courses, guides and pitch databases on her website The Freelancer's Year.

These are all things she first created for herself. And today, almost 90% of her income comes through her online programs, courses and resources – rather than freelance writing.

That's the power of creating once and selling to many. Over and over again.

But before you rush to develop a digital product range, it's important to note 'passive income' is rarely passive. It can take a lot of time to create a product – hundreds of hours, according to many of the product creators I spoke with. Plus time and energy promoting it every single day after you launch. That might be a distraction away from your core business.

So let's invest that time and energy wisely into products people want, products that will enhance your reputation, and products that will protect or accelerate your growth model.

Where do product ideas come from?

Are you having a hard time imagining anyone handing over their credit card for a fragment of your wisdom? I get it. Imposter syndrome is probably the biggest roadblock to turning your knowledge into products. Yet the success of many consultants in this area suggests it's possible.

'There are some absolute genius freelancers out there who have parlayed their skills into a course and community model,' says Rachel Smith, the founder of freelance jobs platform Rachel's List.

Lindy is one example. As a freelance journalist, she started a blog sharing what she was earning every month. Then she started showing them how she did it, which evolved into little courses and then big courses. And then she created a community.

Whether you want your product model to become your core business or not, you have to start somewhere.

First, write down all the very specific problems you solve for your clients. If you're not sure, ask them what problems triggered them to first come to you.

Then, think about how you can share your 'secret sauce' without actually having to do all the work every single time.

This may mean letting go of every assumption you have about how you do what you do. If you're scared of revealing your IP or if you think no one else could possibly do it the way you do, flip that thinking. First, no one else can execute exactly the way you do – so it doesn't matter if you reveal your go-to framework. And secondly, many people could use that framework to solve more problems, even if they tackle it a little differently.

Now, think about any services you subscribe to. From yoga class apps and weekly recipes to mentor group membership – what keeps you hooked? What can you learn from the way they provide value, make it easy or nudge you to keep using their product?

Finally, you're ready to brainstorm some ideas. Focus on your expertise, passions or life experiences, and whittle it down to just one idea that resonates with you.

You don't want to be all things to all people, so make sure it solves a specific problem for a niche. Don't just rush to create a 'me too' product based on the success of someone else.

Here are some formats you could play with:

- **VIP access:** Allow people to book you in for an hour of one-on-one strategic advice, coaching, focused problem-solving or expert training. You should be able to charge more than your usual hourly rate for this privilege.
- **Subscription-based services:** Turn your easy-to-replicate offerings into a monthly fee for service – such as using AI to generate podcast notes and transcripts or social media marketing.
- **Subscription-based products:** Share a new set of resources each week or month via email for a fee.
- **Online training:** This can range from higher value live webinars or workshops via online platforms to on-demand programs or coaching.
- **Toolkits and templates:** Turn your proven processes into downloadable products, such as checklists, spreadsheets, strategic frameworks, calculators – or even software, ebooks and workbooks.
- **Podcasts:** To generate revenue, you'll need sponsorship, advertising or a paid subscription option.
- **Newsletters:** This can be free newsletters with sponsorship or advertising, or a paid subscription.
- **Memberships:** Build a community and create member-only support or experiences for a fee, and provide lifetime access to a library of resources.

- **Tangible products:** These could be printed workshop tools like strategy card decks or worksheets, or t-shirts and stationery.
- **Franchise model:** Sell your processes and systems to similar freelancers with some form of training accreditation plus a subscription fee.

Not all products are revenue-makers

I mentioned earlier that the idea of 'passive' is a myth. Unfortunately, the 'income' part is also not guaranteed. However, products can bring you extra value beyond revenue.

Many people develop products as a marketing strategy. For example, our agency invested time in creating a 14-day writing challenge – a series of emails with one useful tip and an exercise to help people put our own proven techniques to work, plus a private LinkedIn group to share ideas and feedback.

We offer it free because we genuinely want people to be more confident writing at work. It also helps us expand our network and capture more potential leads – both clients and future talent. Plus, it helped us test and learn what it takes to build a product.

Leif Kendall is a freelance copywriter, and also devotes a large amount of his time to running ProCopywriters, an industry alliance in the UK. The organisation's flagship event is the annual CopyCon. Leif admits to me that while his career ambitions never involved running conferences, he gets enormous satisfaction out of bringing people together: 'I learn so much from all the people I meet. But also, I get to pull it all together – brief the designers and developers, write the email communications – and I can see the impact. So often when we freelance, we're removed from the transformation that follows and rarely hear about the results of our contribution. Running ProCopywriters, I have a really direct connection to the work.'

This deep connection is a very rewarding aspect of creating something for yourself.

Turning DIY tools into a win-win

Many professionals are hesitant to give away their trade secrets for a one-time fee as a do-it-yourself option. However, it turns out products can be an awesome awareness-boosting marketing tool.

I asked Nick Parker, inventor of the tone of voice workshop toolkit Voicebox, about the impact his product has had on his business, That Explains Things.

Nick packaged up all his voice know-how, expertise and magic into this product for £699 + VAT.

As a result of the time and effort Nick put into his product – a lot of effort – he became known as the 'tone of voice guy'. More clients came to him because they realised it would be easier if he did it all for them.

The process of making it also sharpened his own thinking and his own creative practice. It forced him to turn his intellectual property into a tangible product – in other words, turned all the years of expertise and ideas floating around in his head into something really useful for others.

Plus, he can have an impact with hundreds of customers all over the world simultaneously without any extra incremental effort.

'I only have a finite amount of time. Having other ways that people can buy my expertise is win-win. Financially, it works,' he says.

That Explains Things is essentially a hybrid model powered by a robust ecosystem of products, with very deliberate boundaries on scope and scale.

Here's how Nick explains his business: 'I'm a company of one, really. I deliberately don't think of myself as a freelancer. That Explains Things is a limited company. I have a brilliant part-time virtual studio manager and occasionally work with a freelancer on projects, but the creative work is mostly just me. I'm the only full-time employee. I'm happy to grow it, but I don't want "headcount".'

Nick had the idea for Voicebox when he was talking to other writers and realised they didn't know how to talk about brand voice to their clients. He began working with a business coach who specialises in productising strategies.

'Julia Chanteray kept me accountable to keep going and gave me some structure around prototyping, iteration and feedback,' he explains. 'I thought, if I can sell a couple of these a month, that will be amazing. It gives my business a strong foundation and keeps everything ticking over. And that's basically what happened. I sell around 20 to 25 a year.'

That's predictable revenue – without having to hustle for projects. But Nick says the value to his business goes beyond cashflow:

> 'Everyone should make a product, because it forces you to articulate what you know and how you can teach it to other people. It may even force you to break new ground in your own thinking.'

'Because of Voicebox, I've probably done more new thinking about tone of voice than anyone in the world,' he says.

Nick worked with Julia again to turn Voicebox into a short online course. That process made him realise a large part of building a product is not about the content – it's about learning how to use the digital platforms you need to create that thing. In his case, video editing software.

He also sends a monthly newsletter, Tone Knob, via Substack. This platform encourages followers to pay a nominal subscription to creators.

By creating this small ecosystem of products, Nick is now in a position where interesting client work finds him, from big corporate gigs to what he describes as 'niche cool stuff'. Clients see him as a strategic thinking partner in writing, which puts him in a strong negotiating position.

'There's no way I'd come in at that level as a copywriter,' he admits.

Nick's investment in a few top-notch products has completely changed the nature of his business. But he is very deliberate about calling his business a studio, because he wants to avoid the expectations that come with being an agency: 'In my experience, saying you're an "agency" often comes with an unspoken sense that you'll say yes to anything, and that "growing the agency" is a marker of quality and success. I didn't want that. To me, a studio is small. It knows what it does. And it does that well.'

Creating a product ecosystem

Julia Chanteray has spent several decades building her own businesses, coaching other businesses and helping others (including Nick) create digital products. She says it's not enough to build one product: you need multiple related products to increase opportunities for customers to buy from you over and over again.

Her own website showcases this approach. She has 'lead magnets' to gain permission to send you emails. These include an interactive quiz and free ebook on the secrets of business success. Then there are 'tripwires' – low-cost tools and guides to build trust in the value of the product, like a pricing ebook or cashflow forecast tool. And then there are the packaged coaching sessions, easily booked online – her core offering.

She suggests adding more premium products, such as mastermind groups, intensive courses, live teaching or personalised assessments.

Building an ecosystem of products also makes it relatively easy to convert your revenue to a recurring subscription fee model – an exclusive membership for access. But again, there is nothing passive about this income stream: members will continue to expect more.

Start with a minimum viable product

Creating an entire shop-full of products might sound daunting. So start by testing the market with a minimum viable product: something that has enough features to be usable and useful, and gives you feedback for further development.

Picture your ideal customer, and remember the specific problem you can help them solve. Before you go all in on an online course, start lean with one unit. Create content to support that product consistently – such as a blog, YouTube video or podcast. And remember to provide lead magnets: generous freebies to encourage people to try your product and share it with others.

I recently spoke with a specialist engineering consultant who saw a need for a quick, low-cost, DIY version of his noise management reports for construction projects. His product started as a spreadsheet. Almost 10 years later, it's one of the leading software tools in the industry – trusted by major infrastructure builders for quick onsite decisions.

It takes discipline to get a product strategy off the ground, but it's easier if you tackle it one small step at a time.

Put aside time every week to work on this side of your business, and make it the best it can be. Because if your ideal audience loves your products, talks about your products and comes back for more, you'll have regular diversified income to provide the foundation for good business growth.

In a podcast with Ed Gandia[35], entrepreneur Shane Sams described the success of his friend's $5 dinner membership site. For US$5 a month, her subscribers receive grocery lists and recipes to make dinners for a family of five on a US$5 budget.

Shane says you either have to put in the focused effort yourself or invest money to outsource and automate parts of the process. 'There's only two ways to be a successful online entrepreneur. You roll up your sleeves or you open your wallet. That's it,' he told Ed.

---

35 b2blauncher.com/episode322.

Services as products

Clients are used to measuring the value of your offering in hours. But what if you flipped this thinking and turned those intangible 'done for you' services into a packaged-up product? This is the challenge Tyler Hakes is now grappling with in his Optimist collective model.

'We are thinking about how we productise specific deliverables and then put them together in different ways to solve different client problems,' he says. 'We've built core deliverables, but now we need to package them up in new ways to meet new client goals.'

Another way to productise your services is to create a premium package like a 'VIP Day' – such as a One Day Brand Sprint or Executive Masterclass. Think about how much value you could package up into a six- or eight-hour day, and how you can create replicable processes to reduce your overall effort. That might include client booking and onboarding, defined pre-work, exercises and tasks, and post-session feedback.

The beauty of this type of product is that you're already doing it. You just need to rethink the way you price it. And by eliminating scope creep, it might just help you take back control of your time as a service provider.

You can also create different levels of service as packaged-up products. Sarah Spence says she wanted to 'make it easy for clients to shop online with us.' As well as a vast product ecosystem of masterclasses and templates, Content Rebels now offers three levels of service, which Sarah describes as 'human plus AI, mostly human, or fully human'.

'The onus is now more on the strategy and the brief. We need to make sure everything is set up correctly – a style guide, a tone of voice guide, knowing who we're talking to,' she says. A human editor will always review the output, and Sarah's team has now evolved to be experts in AI prompting and editing rather than writing.

Here's the kicker: Sarah says she can't remember the last time a client requested a fully human service.

Tools and templates

Content Rebels' template shop gives clients access to all the checklists, calendars and planners Sarah and her team have created over the years to evolve their business. With prices starting at A$5, it's a low-cost way to DIY – but Sarah admits they only get the occasional sale.

'Their value is in the commentary around how to use them, all the things I wish I'd known in the beginning. But we haven't been pumping them really hard,' she says.

Tools and templates may sound like a quick-win product, because you already have them in your business. But with so many free tools and templates available online, you need to show how you can solve a common problem better or faster than any other option – including alternatives that cost nothing at all.

For example, Rachel Smith's go-to job board is a product in its own right with a very specific target audience: other freelance journalists and writers. She shares a wide range of time-saving tools and templates, including lead and pitch tracker spreadsheets, that help them set up the right systems. I happily spent around $5 on her printable to-do list, because it saved me buying a new notepad every two months.

Rachel now offers that to-do list for free, along with some other valuable ebooks and tools, as a lead magnet.

Jordanne Collins also provides a DIY website template product alongside her customised web design, one-week website package and VIP website intensive days.

'Because I am passionate about helping women set up their businesses online, I wanted to offer a more affordable option for those who were hesitant to invest in a custom build,' she explains.

She admits she spent 80 to 100 hours developing the first set of WordPress templates, along with the online store, launch emails and social campaign to support them.

'And I only sold one. I was so disappointed – I'd listened to all the podcasts, read all the books, put in all that time. For one sale. But I knew I could figure out how to make it work, and I spent two more years refining it.'

Jordanne went back to her customers to get direct feedback. She ran surveys, got on the phone and learned what they really needed. She also created video tutorials, checklists and resources for every step: how to do the brand strategy, write copy, set up the website, customise the pages, launch the website.

'I'm glad I didn't give up on the templates because now, when a sale comes in, I get income that I don't have to do any extra work for. It's just there. Plus, I started using the templates myself to create the website-in-a-week offering.'

And those video tutorials also helped her train her growing team to implement the one-week websites. Win–win–win.

The key to this product strategy is to know your audience and solve their problems – rather than just sharing a chunk of your operational process. This also helps you avoid giving your best secrets away to competitors.

Courses and masterclasses

If you already run workshops for clients, running courses might seem like a no-brainer. Create once, sell it forever. Ka-ching!

But it does take time to build and sell an effective online learning program. You'll also need to budget for tech, including learning management systems, video recording software and course marketplaces.

Brooke Hill has experimented with masterclasses and courses as a service extension to her content agency, and she says they take a lot of work.

'I really love doing them, they're fun. But it's not a significant income stream yet,' she says. What they do give her is a channel to share the strategic thinking and services she offers, which she says is a big value add for clients.

You absolutely need credibility in your area of expertise if you're going to convince people to part with hundreds or even thousands of dollars for your training program.

Teaching or coaching others to do things for themselves is a very different skill to doing it for them as a service provider. So, before you start developing a course, spend some time learning how people like to learn.

For example, microlearning modules can be more effective than a 30-minute video – think about super-short snapshot videos with one compelling insight, quizzes and polls, worksheets or calculator widgets.

These steps can help you kick-start your course development:

1. **Build your audience first.** Start sowing the seeds of expectation for your program on social media – and use this as an opportunity to listen to the questions your audience

is asking. Think about the topics and skills you could cover that would help them solve their own challenges. Focus on one outcome – something you could sum up in one sentence. It should be something you know and understand so well, you could talk about it in great detail off the cuff.

2. **Choose an online course platform.** The tech you use will shape the learning experience for your attendees – and also ideally make the course development a seamless experience for you. Look for a platform that combines sales, marketing, video lessons, different course content formats and a solid learning management system all in one.

    You can also use a growing number of AI-enabled tools to help you build the course content. These make it simpler to convert blogs, YouTube videos or podcast episodes into online courses or step-by-step guides.

3. **Price for accessibility, time for completion.** When I develop workshops for clients, I make sure their fee more than covers the time it takes to create a bespoke program.

    However, you can't think like this with an online course.

    Cost will be a barrier to purchase, especially while you are still building trust in your expertise and value. It's better to sell 100 courses at $150 a pop than one (to your mum) at $1499.

    Time can also be a barrier, so keep your course short and practical. If you can teach people something useful in an hour or less, you'll increase your completion rate – and this matters, because if people don't complete the course, they don't see any value.

4. **Get testimonials.** Ask people to tell their friends and colleagues if they enjoyed the course. Then capture and share all the positive testimonials. People are more likely

to trust the words of your customers than your own, so it's a good idea to plan to share at least one testimonial a week if you can – you should see an immediate impact on conversion rates.[36]

5. **Offer post-training support.** Courses can create an easy upsell opportunity. Once people learn the basics, they might realise it's either all too hard and they'd rather pay you to do it for them, or that they need a bit more support – which is where one-on-one coaching comes in.

You could convert your program cohort into a subscription-based community, where they continue sharing learning among themselves and build a valuable network. Or, provide value-adds to encourage course completion, such as a downloadable cheat sheet, framework, spreadsheet or playbook to help them continue applying their new skill in their day-to-day lives.

It's also worth considering live training products as part of your course mix, such as webinars with aligned experts or cohort-based courses where a small 'special' group goes through your program together. They get direct access to you – for a higher fee – as well as the benefits of being part of an exclusive mastermind community.

Memberships and communities

If you've built a valuable network of likeminded colleagues, clients and even competitors over the years, you also have a solid foundation for a product within that community.

Rachel says she grew her online jobs board into a subscription-based membership model quite organically.

---

[36] This is important for everything you sell, not just courses.

'It was originally an email list of journos and colleagues who wanted to stay connected, and then editors heard about it and started sending me jobs,' she explains. In 2012, she set up a website.

Now, her goal for Rachel's List is to make it the place where businesses go to find a writer.

'My cautionary tale is to avoid treating your model as a community service instead of a business,' says Rachel. 'If you start your membership fee too low, it can be hard to lift it.'

She suggests comparing with all the different subscription models out there and thinking about the value you're willing to create and share through different resources.

'There are memberships that give you access to everything for a larger annual fee. We chose a different model, where we create masterclasses and resources that members can add if they want.'

Once Rachel realised she was spending around 40% of her time managing Rachel's List, she decided to price it for the value she was creating. Originally, her first membership fee was just $24.95 a year. Today, it's almost five times that – and more for monthly payments due to the extra admin. But Rachel says it's still very affordable compared with other memberships.

And with over 4000 members, it's clear there is value in the community. Rachel also spends time building a sponsored podcast and annual conference with fellow freelance journalist Lynne Testoni, and uses insights from the community to make sure everything they share is valuable and engaging.

'We have this rich data across three crossover audiences of creatives: Rachel's List, *The Content Byte* podcast and the Summit,' she says. 'We keep a close eye on engagement in our

Facebook group, and on newsletter open rates, and the things people are clicking on repeatedly informs the podcast, the blog at Rachel's List and the summit agenda.'

With all these business streams, Rachel can only spend about half her time on client work – but she says the variety keeps her going. And while the summit event is an all-consuming amount of work, the excitement of bringing together her community is a reward in itself: 'For our first summit, we set a goal to sell a hundred tickets – and we exceeded that. But it doesn't make money. It's really just a massive billboard for the podcast, for Rachel's List, for us as freelancers.'

She says you might not make a large profit from products like events or podcasts, but you need to treat them as an investment in what comes next:

> 'Events bring you opportunities. It's all about the people, the relationships you build, and that can lead to work.'

The Five Ps and productising your business

Our five principles for good business growth also apply to developing a product strategy. Make sure your product range has a clear purpose and you are clear on the value it can bring to your ideal customer. Especially in an internet full of free products-as-marketing-tools.

The more you can create once and use infinitely, the more time you'll have for your core service income streams. As Jordanne and Tyler have found, efficient processes and automated technology are fundamental to creating products that come as close as possible to passive income.

Those systems can also help you delegate product delivery to other people on your team – whether that's video tutorials to support Jordanne's website-in-a-week or the workflow tools Tyler uses to break his productised services into quick tasks.

Systems might also involve setting boundaries. If you keep the scope of your product suite contained and lean, it's easier to stick to a regular schedule of updates and improvements.

And finally, product profitability will ultimately depend on your pricing strategy. This can be a delicate balance to strike – you can price low and focus on mass-marketing tactics, or follow the luxury brand model and price with a VIP or scarcity approach. As Rachel has found, once you set your price it's hard to change without upsetting loyal customers or members.

That's why it's important to understand the numbers first. Think about all the costs of product creation – tech, production and time. Work out how many you think you can sell in a given period and how much profit you want to make.

Here's an example. Let's say you plan to put 100 hours into developing a course, and you value that time at $140 per hour because that's what you could otherwise be earning on billable client work. Your tech and marketing costs add up to $100 per month for software subscriptions and social media marketing.

If you price your course at $250 per person, and aim to sign up 100 people in the first year, you'll make $9800 in profits – a 39% margin. If you think you can charge $1000 per person but only expect 25 people to sign up at that price, you'll make the same $9800 profit.

The right numbers for you will depend on how well known you are for this topic, and the quality and size of your network of target customers.

Are products really worth the effort?

Turning your service-based model into a product-focused model is a mindset shift. It also requires a fair amount of time, energy and discipline to build an ecosystem of products. There are no guarantees that these will create enough revenue to replace your freelance or agency services. The most likely scenario is that it provides a small side-hustle income stream.

However, there are many other benefits to adding products to your mix:

- It can protect your cashflow through economic downturns or industry setbacks by diversifying your customer base.
- You can go deep into a challenge that genuinely interests you and build credibility as an expert in that field.
- You can expand awareness of that expertise beyond your inner circle of clients, opening the door to other marketing opportunities such as speaking gigs or podcasts.

Products can also become a tangible part of the value of your business – which can make you a more interesting proposition to potential acquirers if you're thinking about your exit strategy. One day, you might decide that you're ready to move on, and we'll cover those options in chapter 11.

But before we start thinking about handing over the reins to your business, it's time for a quick reality check. Because even with your Five Ps in place and the best of intentions, you will encounter a few obstacles on the way to good business growth. Let's look at how to get back on track in the next chapter.

 ARE YOU READY TO SELL PRODUCTS?

The set-and-forget income model might be right for you if:

- ✓ you're willing to invest time and money into creating and testing a product or subscription service
- ✓ you could solve a common problem or share your valuable IP without having to do all the work
- ✓ there is potential marketing upside in your product idea, as well as revenue
- ✓ you want to create something tangible – whether that's a card set or a community.

The set-and-forget income model might *not* be right for you if:

- ✗ you are unsure what your market needs
- ✗ you don't have time to test and learn.

LET'S GROW

Got a rock-solid idea for an evergreen product? Write it down now!

1. What tools, templates or frameworks have you already created for yourself (or a client) that others would pay for?

   ....
   ....
   ....
   ....
   ....
   ....
   ....
   ....

2. What's the first step you can take to testing that product? How will you find and build your target audience?

   ....
   ....
   ....
   ....
   ....
   ....
   ....
   ....

Good growth is **about thriving**. Not just surviving.

10: The good growth reality check

Sustaining your mojo when the going gets tough

Over the last six chapters, we've explored many different ways to grow beyond solo on your terms. And hopefully, you feel more confident about what's next and how to get there.

But before you get carried away imagining just how much bigger and better you could be, here's the uncomfortable truth:

Scaling growth in a service business is hard.

By scaling growth, I mean those 10× revenue models embraced by tech companies and venture capitalists. I've worked through some scaling up frameworks, and while they have some solid ideas for building a strong foundation, their pathways don't feel realistic for a business so dependent on talent.

Perhaps that's because my idea of good business growth is not the same as Amazon's or Airbnb's.

For many years, my business growth plateaued – no matter how hard I worked. I felt stuck and wondered what I was doing wrong. When I started to think about what good growth really meant to me, I was able to flip that mindset.

> A flat horizontal line can also mean stability and predictability. A micro business can be a mature business.

That might feel like a radical idea in a world that always demands *more*.

However, as we've established, good growth is about thriving. Not just surviving.

If we think about what growth means outside business revenue or profits, it's never infinite. At a certain point, bodies stop growing. Trees put down stable roots and mature. Untamed cellular growth in the human body has a name: cancer.

So, before we go any further, it's time to draw a line in the sand. Back in chapter 3 we talked about defining what is *enough*. What will make you feel like you (and the people around you) are thriving?

Yes, this is a number – a certain income level or profit share, or how many employees or clients you work with. But it's also what that number lets you do, like put your kids through school or take a five-week holiday every year. Don't worry if it doesn't feel realistic: just writing that goal down is a way of setting that intention.

Up isn't the only way

Economic and management theory suggests growth is always an upward trajectory. But real life is messy and unpredictable, and people are not machines.

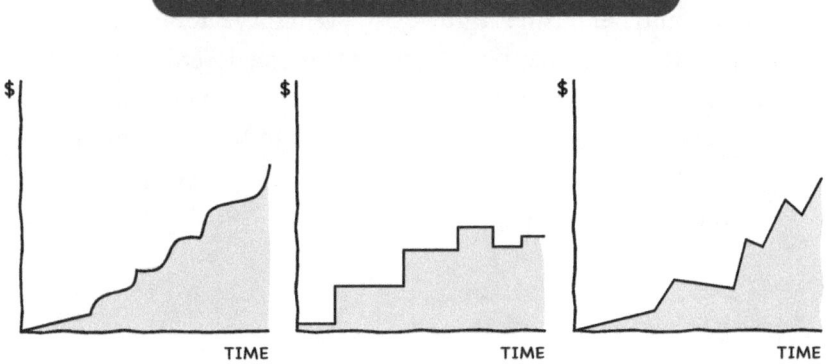

There will be times when, despite your best intentions, your purpose, proposition, people and processes aren't delivering the profit you imagined. It can be hard to sustain your mojo when projects stall, budgets get slashed or your most loyal clients are made redundant.

Those things have all happened to my business while I've worked on this book. That meant working through budget scenarios B, C and D, and making some tough decisions.

It's reassuring to know I'm not alone in dealing with these challenges. Many business owners are exhausted. We've been pinballing from crisis to crisis. What we all crave is a bit of control.

Reframing flatlining revenue as within your control can help. As long as the business beneath it is sustainable. Marketing agency founder Janine Pares says she defines good growth as something that looks stable and under control:

> 'There's the excitement and energy that comes from a frenetic period, but that's rarely sustainable.'

At one point, her business grew 100% year on year. But she admits that was a crazy time. Today, when she describes a good business, it's all about maturity: retaining the right people, trusting that things will get done when you're not in the room, and providing a consistent client experience when you add new things into the mix.

Take control where you can

If your external environment is dealing you a few up-and-down wildcards, you need to take control where you can. Here are some small changes you can make to do just that.

Strengthen the relationships that matter

Economic downturns, client budget shifts and restructures are all factors outside your control. But you can control the way you respond.

If your favourite client is made redundant, keep that person engaged as part of your network. Especially if they're going through a hard time after losing their job – you'd be surprised how few people reach out and ask how they can help. And you can bet those are the people they'll turn to first when they do land on their feet.

If you have a loyal client who is a consistent advocate for you, thank them with a surprise lunch, spa treatment or gift card. That person is your unpaid sales rep, and you don't even need to manage their performance.

Invest in one big thing

If your lead pipeline is starting to look a little dry, is there one thing you could do differently? When time and money are scarce, it may be better to put all your effort into one big attention-grabbing idea than spread yourself thin over endless prospecting emails or social posts.

Sponsoring a B2B marketing conference is Janine's one big-ticket marketing tactic. With events in Sydney, Melbourne and Singapore, she says the conference helps her lift the awareness of her business and the breadth of the agency's capabilities: 'We're a small player in a big pond. So, this is super important for building awareness and levelling out the playing field. It's a significant investment, but it's the only thing we spend money on.'

Janine uses her sponsorship to get on stage and share her knowledge: 'That's really how we build relationships, and it's based on ongoing engagement.'

She says she's acquired long-term clients this way, but it can be a slow burn – in some cases taking up to two years to convert. It's not a quick-fix-in-a-crisis strategy, but it may be the thing that sets you up for more stable, controlled growth in the next few years.

Pay attention to the little things

Long-term success is the result of thousands of tiny steps. Big changes feel hard and are easy to procrastinate over. But if you could do one sales-driving activity every day for just 15 minutes – create one social post, create one email newsletter, follow up one lapsed lead – you'd be more likely to see a return on time invested sooner.

Are there any tiny gaps in your client experience or processes? Fix them. That might be as simple as a smarter PowerPoint template, or an automated calendar booking system, or a referral reward program.

If the solution doesn't exist, build it. One minimum viable product step at a time. Because if you're feeling it, there's a chance others are too – and that could end up being your productised ticket to recurring revenue.

Attend big-ticket events

Powerful relationships can start with a single conversation. Industry events are a great place to chat with likeminded peers, and it's a lot easier and more affordable to attend an event than sponsor it.

I've picked up a major corporate client in a coffee queue. That person went on to refer us into another major corporate when she jumped ship. Combined, that five-minute conversation generated around 20% of our revenue at one point.

Carolyn Loton says all her health sector work stems from a random conversation in the lunch line at an industry event. It's now a sizeable proportion of her business.

There are no guarantees with this tactic, but you're at least likely to learn something about your industry. Apart from time, what have you got to lose?

Sharpen up your service stories

Are your most valued services also your best-kept secret? When you're busy running your business, it's easy to assume your clients know all the things you do well.

But often they really have no idea unless you explicitly go out there and tell them.

Brooke Hill says she's added many new services to Wonderthink's offering, including helping her clients work with AI: 'But the services we've always offered – consulting, coaching and content – are still our core, and I think we're getting better at talking about them.'

Writing a case study about a project that went well or a service you love providing is also a great opportunity for positive self-reflection. So, put a tiny bit of time into case studies, videos, social posts or pitch decks that bring those services to life, and start talking about them. Relentlessly.

Make the hard decisions

The pace of change is never going to slow down. So, if your business model has been disrupted by technology, upstart competitors, global tensions or regulatory change, don't hide under the doona pining for the way things were.

Take a hammer to your breakeven model. Pull it apart. And put it back together again with a realistic target that protects your interests.

This is what it takes to be agile as a small business. And it might mean making tough calls, like letting people go. That really hurts. But if the alternative means putting everyone else's livelihoods at risk (including yours), it might be your only option.

It might also mean resetting expectations for how you work as a team. For a long time, I thought I had to be the only one who'd step up and take on the extra hours. If hard things had to be done, and especially if they had to be done after hours, I thought that was all on me. If the office cleaner couldn't come, I'd mop the floors. If a client call needed to be made at 9 pm, I'd put my hand up. If an urgent job required the weekend ... yep, that was on me too.

That's not sustainable for any human. It can also fuel a truckload of resentment over time. As Janine puts it, 'working in a small business does ask more of people. They have to be more versatile and have initiative. You've got to just get things done and not be too precious. We all have to muck in.'

What might it look like if you stopped bending over backwards to make things as easy as possible for your team? You are still offering them a trade-off: while you expect them to muck in – all hands on deck – they get full autonomy and flexibility.

Hard decisions could involve letting clients go too. An 'energy vampire' who sucks your day dry is often the root cause of general frustration or overwork. Sending them elsewhere will free you and your team to focus on higher-calibre work.

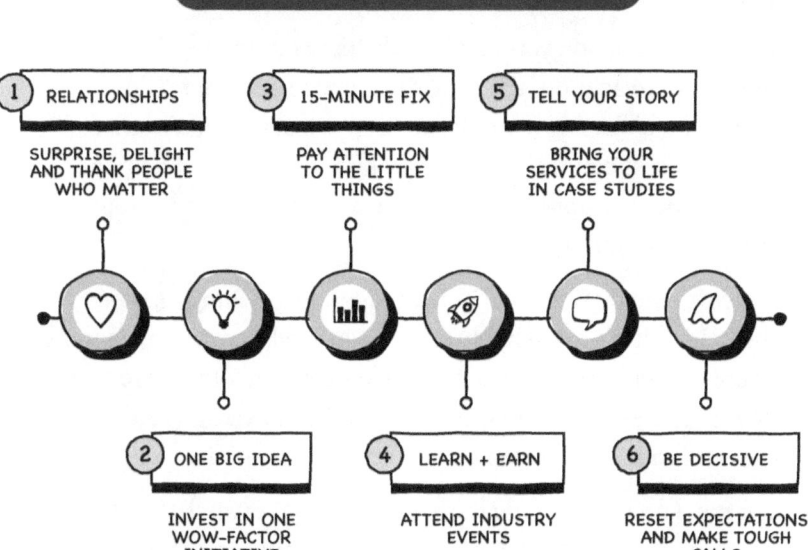

Be kind to yourself

In 2022–23, accounting platform Xero asked over 4600 small business owners in seven countries about their psychological wellbeing.[37] As well as finding small business owners experience lower levels of wellbeing than the general population, the survey also revealed over a third experience financial distress at least more than half the time. Almost half also said stress from work invades their personal lives at least more than half the time.

---

37 'The Global State of Small Business Owner Wellbeing', Xero, November 2022 through to February 2023.

There's no doubt external factors beyond our control – from a global pandemic to persistent inflation – have made it a tough time to run a small business. Relentless pressure and setbacks can make it tricky to sustain your own motivation, let alone keep your team inspired.

But before you pop yourself into the burnout bucket, it's important to acknowledge the difference between feeling stressed and feeling overwhelmed. I've learned that a small dose of stress can turbocharge my effectiveness and help me push through. There is nothing like a hard deadline to stop me procrastinating.

However, if you feel incapable of tackling anything on your to-do list, that's more likely to mean overwhelm. Well-meaning people might offer to help, but you can't figure out where to even begin. In these moments, you need to acknowledge you're doing the best you can and step away from whatever it is.

For me, I need to still my mind in the face of overwhelm. That might mean going on a long, quiet walk. Your reset tactic might be different – perhaps it's dancing, or drawing, or meditating. Find your thing, and give yourself permission to make time for it.

Your business, your team and your relationships will be all the better for it. And remember, you chose this path because you wanted to work on your terms – not those of your manager or shareholders.

Keep going

When running your business feels like a struggle, it might be tempting to give up and walk away. However, you've worked hard to get to this point. And you may have set up some structures and staffing models that are difficult (and expensive) to unravel.

That's why it helps to plan some possible exit points on your growth journey. You don't have to take that turnoff, but knowing it is just ahead can help you get through the challenging times.

You'll also enjoy a much better chance of walking away with some financial upside if you plan your finish line. We'll take a realistic look at what that takes in the next chapter.

✱ TAKE ACTION

Do you need a mojo reset? Here's a quick recap. Just choose one idea: you truly don't need anything else on your plate right now.

- [ ] Define your 'enough' target and get clear on why it matters to you – what does it allow you to do?
- [ ] Make more time for the clients who feed your energy. Those are the relationships you can count on when the going gets tough.
- [ ] Invest in one big marketing push, or sign up for one big industry event.
- [ ] Set aside 15 minutes every single day for one small lead-boosting task. Write that social post. Fix that workflow. Send that newsletter. You'll never regret it.
- [ ] What's one amazing project you've loved working on this year? Write a case study. Showcase that service.
- [ ] If there's someone in your team or on your client books who is draining your energy, weigh up the impact of letting them go.
- [ ] Give yourself space and time away from the causes of stress. Even if it's just 10 minutes.
- [ ] Give yourself a future way out by planning your exit strategy.

LET'S GROW

Come back to these notes whenever you feel like things aren't quite going according to plan.

1. What numbers define 'enough' for you? Think annual income or percentage revenue growth, number of staff or number of clients. What will that number allow you to do?

   ....
   ....
   ....
   ....

2. What is the biggest cause of stress or overwhelm in your business right now?

   ....
   ....
   ....
   ....

3. What is one thing you can do to deal with this?

   ....
   ....
   ....
   ....

NOTES

Define your final destination, and take control of the last leg of your business journey.

11: Beyond solo to exit strategy

Getting the most from your business when it's time to move on

Most people don't start a business with the end in mind. In the adrenalin rush of acquiring that first client, we're probably not also thinking about setting our businesses up for acquisition.

Running a business often feels like a marathon with no finish line in sight. But here's the thing: *you* get to define that finish line. And if you do that well, you can get more value from your business than the money you make month on month, year on year.

I asked every person I spoke with, solopreneur or agency owner, whether they had an exit strategy. Only one said yes – and he's already well on his way through his succession plan.

Most freelancers shared the feeling that having an exit plan would lock them into an approach that might not work for them in three, five or ten years' time. Similarly, they were also reluctant to plan their business three, five or ten years ahead. The freedom of freelancing, for them, meant always being open to opportunities they can't yet foresee.

'I don't even have a three-, five- or ten-year plan,' Amy Ragland says. 'I don't ever want to miss out on something because I was locked into my plan. And sometimes we make big plans or set big goals and life happens.'

In contrast, agency owners agreed they need to build something that has more value than just providing them with a job. And one day, they'd like to walk away with that value.

That's how they define financial freedom.

However, finding time for strategising your end game when you're busy putting out fires every single day, bending to the whims of clients and managing the emotions of your team can sometimes feel impossible.

For any business owner, an exit typically comes down to one of three options: an external sale (or merger), an internal succession plan or simply closing the doors.

Stop, succession or sell

There are plenty of stories about how businesses get started. But very few about how they end. That's probably because the majority simply stop.

Stop

Over half a million small businesses in the US close every year.[38] The number shutting down shop due to insolvency is growing – in Australia by as much as 20% in 2024[39] – and 15% of small and mid-sized UK companies are at risk of insolvency.[40]

Insolvency is not how you want your business story to end.

But if you don't think consciously about what the final stage looks like for you, it's more likely that one day you'll decide you've had enough. That decision might be forced on you through ill health or other personal circumstances. And you'll simply stop taking on projects and start winding things down.

To be quite frank, there is nothing wrong with this. Remember, good growth is about defining what is enough. If you feel you've had enough, that's okay. As long as you feel in control of your destination.

---

38 chamberofcommerce.org/small-business-statistics: around 595,000 businesses fail or close each year.
39 Illion Commercial Risk Barometer, 2024.
40 Allianz Global Insolvency Outlook: Reality check.

Ed Gandia suggests freelancers keep a separate account for retained earnings that effectively becomes their retirement plan. 'You could build a nest egg over the course of 15 to 20 years. Then, when you decide to hang up your hat, you already have the equivalent of selling your business.'

He has consciously decided he won't create a five-, ten- or 25-year plan because he needs some of his journey to be spontaneous.

A nest egg is a smart approach if you have the discipline to put aside a decent chunk of profit every year. It's harder to do when you also want to pay the mortgage and take a family vacation.

So, let's explore some of the alternative endings for the choose-your-own-adventure story that is your business.

Succession

While I was working on this book, I was also working on a succession plan for Writers. During a few periods of overwhelm and exhaustion, I had come close to walking away from the business I had spent so much time, energy and love creating – but I was determined not to let it end that way.

I always wanted to build a business that could thrive without me. So, my approach is to sell from within. For my team to take on some equity in the business as well as more responsibility.

From formal staff equity plans to less formal management transitions, there are many different ways to transfer ownership and responsibility for your business to someone within your team.

The biggest hurdle is finding the right person. But if you've focused on attracting the right talent to your team – the do-ers who care as much about your purpose, proposition, people and profitability as you do – then you may find the solution is staring right at you.

As Seth Godin said on the *Built to Sell* podcast, 'Your job is to find other people to do all the jobs. If you keep hiring yourself to do the work, you're hiring the cheapest, most available, most overworked person in the organisation. That doesn't scale.'[41]

A few years ago, one of our writers asked me if I'd be willing to sell 20% of the business equity to her. Nikola had been weighing up whether to keep pursuing her own freelance side hustle while working part-time for us, and then realised the business she really wanted to run was the one she was already in.

This was very good news, because I'd consciously thought about Nikola as my potential successor from her first day on the team.

The process took longer than we expected, even though we were already coming from a place of trust. The first step was to get a formal valuation and agree a number. With the help of our accountants, we found the simplest solution was for Nikola to borrow money from the business to pay for the equity. She'd then pay that interest-free loan back over five years, ideally using dividends.

There are a few restrictions on how your company can finance equity purchases in Australia, and you'll need accounting, tax and legal advice before you can set up this structure. But as it's unlikely your staff have sizeable savings ready to invest, it's a relatively accessible option. Alternatives include external funding (such as from a bank). Or you can give a portion of equity away – although it's likely you'll end up paying tax on that gift.

---

41 Seth Godin, 3 May 2024, builttosell.com/radio/episode-440.

Tyler Hakes says he can see a scenario where he could slowly step away from Optimist and somebody else on the team could run things. 'We would simply reconfigure how that profit gets distributed. While we haven't formalised any plans yet, we have talked about this more broadly,' he says.

Having those conversations plants a seed in your potential successor's mind. It also forces you to consciously start letting go.

Pitstop owner Georgi Roberts didn't start her digital marketing agency: she was the original founder's succession plan. After contracting for the small agency to see if it was the right fit, she initially bought 25% equity. And then acquired another 24% to bring her share to just under half.

'I don't know why I didn't go all in and buy 49% straightaway. It cost me more in the end!' she says.

Georgi and Pitstop founder Penelope enjoyed splitting the responsibilities, and Georgi loved the feeling of being in control over business decisions after working in government for many years. However, it all came suddenly to a head when Penelope was offered a lucrative job by a client and decided to step away.

There wasn't much time for a handover, and rushing the transaction ended up being, in Georgi's words, 'messy, with an unexpected tax bill'. Six years later, she has more than doubled the size of the agency and is now looking at her own exit strategy options. This time, she's making sure she has plenty of time to nurture a potential successor, build up a network of potential acquirers and create a platform for her next venture.

Georgi's experience highlights the value of planning an equity-enabled succession plan carefully. Here are some steps to consider.

1. **Start with some seriously honest conversations.**
   A successful business partnership is like a successful marriage – so first, you need to make sure you both want the same things. Think about your own goals. How much equity and control do you want to keep? What do you want the next few years to look like personally – do you want to work fewer hours, or have more flexibility?

   Have some robust discussions about how you will divvy up leadership and management responsibilities within the business:

   - Are you both on board with the business strategy and targets?
   - How will you define your roles and responsibilities?
   - How will you make big decisions together?
   - What skills will your new co-director or partner need to develop to take on more?
   - Do you need to reset salary packages?
   - What happens if the business starts to experience financial problems?

2. **Understand your succession options.** Instead of a straightforward equity sale, you could set up a staff equity plan as part of your rewards package. For example, you could give staff the choice to buy shares in the business at a discounted price and/or with their pre-tax salary. You could also give the shares away as 'bonus' remuneration for high performance. Or you could create a share options scheme, where all eligible employees have the right to buy shares at a preset price – in some cases this price could be zero – within a set time period.

   Why would employees want those shares? There is one critical P you need in place before you start setting up any kind of incentive plan: *profit*. Your team is unlikely to welcome this initiative with any level of enthusiasm unless there is a realistic and regular pot of money ready to be divvied up.

If you are profitable, staff could earn dividends as well as salary. These schemes also give them a stake in your future successful business. If your exit strategy includes an acquisition, their shares could turn into money in the bank. Major shareholders may also have greater decision-making rights.

Share schemes won't appeal to all employees. Some people prefer a regular paycheque without worrying about what is driving the business. And that's okay.

However, for the right people, an equity plan can be a great incentive to work on the business as well as in the business. It strengthens a culture of accountability and ownership. Just make sure you align the allocation of share options or equity earn out with clear, measurable performance targets. For example, growing client revenue in specific industries or markets that person has responsibility for.

There are many different ways to set these sorts of schemes up, but check the regulations in your country first to make sure they're both legal and tax effective. It's so important to get professional external advice – there are many decisions to make in this process, and they will impact your business structure, agreements, tax and team morale.

When we were going through this process, we were advised to keep it simple. We also learned creating a share program in a business at this size is probably overkill. From an incentive point of view, we were better off setting up a clear, transparent profit pool bonus scheme – so everyone who helps the business succeed benefits in some way from that success.

3. **Get an external valuation.** You've identified the right person to take on ownership. You've worked out a simple entry process. But you can't start negotiating terms until you agree what the business is currently worth.

   This can be an enlightening exercise. It makes you think like an investor rather than a business owner.

   There are many different ways to arrive at a market value. Typically, it's based on a set multiple of a financial number, most commonly one of:

   - EBITDA – earnings before income tax and depreciation (similar to profit)
   - revenue
   - assets.

   Multiples vary widely – some industries (such as high-growth tech start-ups) might report multiples of 5× or even 10× EBITDA. For small creative agencies, that number could be less than 1× revenue, or around 1 to 2× EBITDA.

   Other factors may increase your valuation, including:

   - recurring revenue (the more, the better)
   - revenue growth rate in the last year (ideally, a consistent upward trajectory)
   - key employee turnover (are you keeping your best people?)
   - profit margin (is in it line with industry benchmarks?)
   - competitive advantages (what do you have or do that others cannot match?)
   - customer concentration (is there a risk of losing your main revenue source?)
   - strength of management team (how experienced, capable and committed are you?)

- business processes (how robust are your policies, contracts and IT systems?)
- growth opportunities (do you have what it takes to keep growing?).

If you think you might want to sell your business at any time in the future, these levers should be part of your strategy.

4. **Update your shareholders' agreement.** You'll need a lawyer to help you with this one. They should ask how you and any other directors want to make decisions about things like:
   - how shareholders can sell or transfer shares
   - what happens if one shareholder dies
   - how the market value of shares is determined in the future
   - how company income is distributed
   - how much notice retiring or exiting shareholders must give
   - who has ultimate control or veto over management decisions.

   Being a shareholder is very different to being an employee: it comes with certain obligations and responsibilities. So, think carefully about some potential worst-case scenarios and how you'd handle them together. As our adviser told us, 'Everyone has a right to fly in the plane, but not everyone should be the pilot.'

5. **Start letting go.** You have someone else now to help you work out which route to take on the next stage of your business journey. Their job is also to start wearing some of the many different hats that have been weighing you down. Nikola quickly took a large amount of HR and team

management tasks off my to-do list and became the face of Writers for a growing number of clients.

This freed me to focus on what I did best – a gift for any overstretched business owner – but it also made me realise how many small but important tasks and processes were held by me.

Think of your succession plan as an entry strategy for your successor, not an exit strategy.

Make a list of all the things that only you know how to do. Think of it as your 'hit by a bus' list – what would stop happening if you couldn't turn up to work tomorrow? Then, start handing those things over. At least one other person in your team needs to know how things get done, from paying staff and renewing subscriptions to running workshops.

The minute I stopped thinking about a succession plan as an exit strategy and started thinking of it as an entry strategy for my successor, it became a whole lot easier to let this stuff go. It also freed me to begin imagining how my role could evolve.

Your exit strategy doesn't need to be an immediate severance. You could still play a role as an adviser, mentor, coach, rainmaker – or help consult on the types of client work you love most.

When content agency founder Matt Fenwick decided he was ready to step back from running True North Content, he started looking for a buyer. He quickly found one within his own business: content strategist Sandra Muller.

As part of the deal, Matt has committed to supporting Sandra for three months, for about an hour a week, and still plays a business development and strategic advice role.

Having worked with Matt for eight years, Sandra says she wasn't ready to let go of the True North Content family.

'I think everyone felt that too, because once word got out that I was one of the preferred buyers there was a collective sense of relief that we get to stay together,' she says.

The idea of starting again and building an agency on her own would have been daunting: 'I've got something fairly epic to start from now, and I can build up other sides of the business like training. That would have been much harder if I was starting from scratch.'

Succession downsides

Before you start pinning all your hopes on an equity buyout as your way out, it's time for a reality check. The truth is, the returns to the founder in this scenario are relatively modest.

Exit Advisory Group founder and business strategy consultant Simon Bedard says many employees just can't afford to buy in.

'A lot of people have ideas that divesting internally will be a beautiful way to keep the business alive and bring people on the journey. But there's a disconnect between what the owner wants personally and what can realistically happen,' he says.

He suggests giving staff shares over a period of time as phantom equity or performance-related incentives to bring people on the journey with you. That might involve allocating the equivalent of 1% of shares per annum over five years in a formal agreement, which might be offset by the dividends they would have earned, or as a performance bonus.

In certain cases, where the valuation fundamentals are sound, banks may be willing to lend staff the funding to buy in as an equity partner. But the security often involves personal assets, such as the family home.

That might not feel realistic for the next generation of employees. Buying in might not be a priority if they're already struggling to afford their first home deposit, mortgage repayments or the costs of raising a family.

Simon emphasises the importance of knowing why you want to exit. What you want to get out of it at the end – a tangible number. And then figuring out the best way to achieve that:

> 'Your business is an asset. It should be helping you deliver the lot – the type of work you want to do, and the financial returns you need now and in the future.'

Keeping it in the family

For some business owners, the 'sell from within' strategy might mean selling or transferring ownership to the next generation, as Peter Fuller has done by handing over the reins to his son, daughter and daughter-in-law.

While he never planned to develop a multi-generational business, his brand communications agency was always a family affair. His wife Kathryn took on the General Manager role, and their kids grew up stuffing conference satchels and running errands at events.

'It is one thing to work in a family business, and another to expect they will take over and devote their lives to it,' says Peter.

He recommends seeking advice from a professional body that specialises in family succession plans, such as the Family Business Association in Australia. They recommend planning early for succession.

'This includes finding a qualified mentor or coach, and meeting frequently to share your dreams and fears,' Peter says.

'Set up a board to oversee the business, write a constitution, establish rules and codes of conduct and commit to an organisational chart so everyone knows where they fit.'

When it comes time for the trickiest bit – the transfer of ownership – use an experienced accountant and solicitor to value the business, and then negotiate a plan to either pay out the current generation or manage their succession.

Peter's post-succession role showcases the possibilities of planning pre-retirement with a sense of purpose and letting the next generation do their thing.

'Most of my friends at this age don't want to retire and stop their lives abruptly. They want a kind of hybrid existence where you can choose your level of "busy-ness",' he explains.

He now has a varied 'background' role, combining writing (which he still loves) with a position as Executive Chair and overseeing the agency's 'For Good' initiatives such as B Corp certification.

'I also have a vaguely defined "cultural ambassador" role, which might mean wandering the building and having random chats with people, or one-on-one mentoring,' he adds.

Mostly, Peter works from his home office, overlooking the family's vineyard in the Barossa, several days a week. He also has the time to play golf, travel, garden and work on his novel while feeling financially secure.

'That, to me, defines success,' he says.

Sell

Fuller recently acquired a smaller agency in Sydney. It was a strategic move, expanding the firm's client base and market research capabilities. It also enabled the exit strategy of the acquired agency's founder.

Many owners, if they think about exit strategies at all, would probably like to one day sell their business. Typically, that might involve a merger or acquisition – selling equity or complete ownership to another agency in the same space, or to a client, or to a different type of business that would like to bolt on your services.

It might seem the simplest solution when you want to walk away – but the reality can be quite different.

Let's start with the numbers. If you're wondering how much your business is worth to a buyer, the answer is probably less than you think. Unlike 10-figure tech deals, when creative agencies are bought (or merge), they are less likely to make headlines.

And when markets are tough, mergers are more likely to be struggling agencies absorbed by stronger ones – with little money changing hands.

However, when planned carefully, a modest acquisition deal can still be a potentially life-changing event.

For example, theygotacquired.com shares the story of a US online training business that was bought by an online content platform. Five years after the founder decided it was time to exit, she sold her business for $4.5 million, 10% of which went to the CEO she hired to get the business to a sale-worthy state. With over 300,000 email subscribers and monthly revenue of $250,000 to $300,000, the business had tangible, profitable value.[42]

Timing is everything

'The most critical aspect to getting a deal done is a willing buyer and a willing seller, who can form a lot of trust in a short period of time,' says Simon Bedard. But while the deal itself might happen quickly, it's usually the result of several years of planning.

'I'm often asked, how soon should I start before I get out?' he says. 'I'd say, a minimum of three years. If you want to stop working in three years, you need time to make a difference to your business first. If it will require a fundamental strategy change, it could take two or three years to prove it – to start showing results. And then you might also need to stick around for a year as part of the deal.'

The other factor is timing. 'The best time to sell a company is when there are more buyers than sellers,' Simon observes. That doesn't happen by accident.

Think about your business with a buyer's mindset. If they are thinking about an acquisition, it's usually due to one or more of these strategies:

- add new clients, fast
- bring on specialist talent
- move into a new geographic market
- diversify revenue in new service areas
- remove competitors from the market.

---

42 theygotacquired.com/content/proofread-anywhere-acquired-by-onfolio-holdings.

When there's a strategic motivation – for example, your business has something unique that would take the buyer years to replicate organically – the multiple they're willing to pay will be higher.

Simon Bedard is conscious of building his own business into a saleable asset. For him, that means addressing the 'key person risk' of being an owner by systemising every aspect of his service delivery: 'For example, we run a regular three-day State of the Market series. We've mapped every single micro-step involved in delivering an event like this. There's a project plan with deliverables and dependencies, which means we know exactly how many hours are involved, and what knowledge and experience is required to complete each task.'

This means Simon can start stepping back from some of the day-to-day responsibilities and keep doing the things he loves – like speaking at events – while his team manages the rest.

'You don't want to transfer key person risk from yourself to someone else,' he notes. 'That's just pushing the issue further down the line. Put in systems so more than one person can make the magic happen.'

Towards a conscious uncoupling

Acquisitions are risky and time-consuming – and the majority of major acquisitions fail post-integration.[43] Staff leave, systems don't work well together, clients feel neglected. The work you do before signing the deal is really important, so if you are approached by a buyer, be very clear about the business and culture fit.

---

43 'Don't Make This Common M&A Mistake', Graham Kenny, *Harvard Business Review*, March 2020.

It's likely that the terms will require you to stay on for at least one or two years after the deal. There will be a financial incentive to do so: for example, you might receive 60% of the purchase price upfront and the balance over a two-year period. You will probably also have a non-compete clause preventing you from taking clients with you after that period ends.

All this can be a difficult experience for a business founder. If you've built a business where your team feels like family, selling your company might feel like a painfully slow relationship breakdown where you have to leave the kids behind.

Or maybe you can see those kids as grown-ups. It's time to let them do their own thing.

If you are planning to be acquired, get clear about your personal goals during that transition period. You might want to learn as much as you can about managing a bigger and more complex business, or broaden your network, to set yourself up for the next big idea. You might need a coach to help you work through what you want personally. Or you might want to focus on supporting your team to make sure they're set up to succeed in whatever that new entity looks like.

Those things are all still within your control, even if your business is no longer yours.

Exploring all your exit options

Defining your finish line is a conscious act, but you don't need to get too specific about dates and times. Once you know what your ideal scenario looks like, be open to different opportunities and connections.

Those connections are the key: it's another person, not a faceless entity, who will buy into your business. As you build strong working relationships with others, think about whether they would fit your ideal buyer or successor profile.

Rachel Smith says she sees Rachel's List as having 'more of an evolution strategy rather than an exit strategy. I can't imagine selling or closing it, but perhaps it could evolve again into something else.'

She admits she wouldn't want to stop freelance writing. Ever. 'I am stocking my super (pension) away in a kind of feverish way that I never did when I was younger, but I see myself at 80 still tapping away, creating something because that's really what drives me.'

Having spent many years building value into their business, agency owners like Sarah Spence are more likely to have a clearer picture of their end game.

'I'm figuring out how to better shore up the business for sale,' she says. 'But I am conscious of "why". It can't just be about money and it's not because I'm frustrated – because if you could fix the things you find frustrating about your business, why would you sell it? It's more about time. It would feel better for my heart if I had more time for the things I don't have capacity for at the moment.'

Sarah has a clear picture in her mind of what that post-exit time might look like. And she already has a potential succession candidate in mind within her business.

Marketing agency owner Janine Pares also has an exit strategy in mind. She's purposefully built her business into a boutique agency capable of competing at the big end of agency town.

'We've got big multinational clients, and we do big work for them,' she says. 'Right now, I'm focused on the next stage of scaling and growing by investing in people, systems and operations.'

Collective owner Tyler Hakes says he thinks Optimist will continue to exist as it is.

'We've had many people approach us with some kind of an acquisition or merger offer. But it's not built to sell. Because there's not that much to sell, right? All the conversations I've had boil down to a situation where "we're going to give you a tiny bit of money and then you work for us for three years". That doesn't sound very fun.'

Simon Bedard suggests thinking of your exit as the off ramp on a freeway.

'Every freeway has logical exit ramps built in along the journey. Unless you are literally at the end of the road, there's more than one option, so understand where your next few exit ramps are likely to appear. Because the way you feel about the journey might change tomorrow.'

> A natural exit ramp could be a business milestone, like the end of a good financial year, or the signing of a three-year client contract.

Clearly, this is a very personal decision. For me, it's important to feel in control of that conscious choice to step away. I've proven to myself that I can grow a company. And now, I can choose not to keep doing it, and choose the next opportunity to do really good work – whatever that might be.

Here are a few thought starters to help you weigh up your exit ramp options:

1. What would you like your life to look like if you weren't running your business?
2. How much money would you need to get out of the business to feel secure in that life?
3. Where is the value in your business right now:
   - Consistent profitability?
   - Recurring revenue?
   - Robust systems and process?
   - Ownable intellectual property, such as frameworks, software or methodology?

Remember, you can't sell your way out of an unprofitable business. So, working backwards from an exit plan can help you define a sustainable business model – and a strategy for good business growth.

LET'S GROW

Whether you want to one day exit your business or keep working as long as you can, take a few minutes to jot down your first thoughts on these questions.

1. What exit option makes most sense to you and your situation: stop, sell or succession plan? Why?

   ....
   ....
   ....
   ....

2. If you'd like to one day sell your business, what type of business or individual could you see taking it over? Make a note of anyone in your network who might be a likely candidate.

   ....
   ....
   ....
   ....

3. What is one thing you could change about your business to enhance its saleable value? For example, increasing recurring revenue, documenting processes, or registering or trademarking IP.

   ....
   ....
   ....

NOTES

You've come so far. And **you are in control of where you go next**.

12: The next step

Ready to make good growth happen for you?

By now I hope you have a clearer idea of how your business can help you enjoy a good life. You've defined what good growth feels like to you – and why you want to take that path.

It might be to stretch yourself personally – to push yourself to do more, learn more and be more.

It might be to solve more problems for your clients – by expanding your skills and services, or increasing your availability.

It might be because you don't want your people to outgrow you. You want to give them the opportunities they need to grow, develop and thrive. Or it might be to create something that will outlive you. And perhaps extract extra value from once you feel ready to wrap things up.

It shouldn't only be about money, although being profitable matters.

Instead, it could be taking all the things you love about freelancing or consulting and making your work better – not just bigger.

Avoiding a growth hangover

Someone once told me business growth can be intoxicating. When times are good, it's easy to get a little drunk on success.

And that's when ego steps in and demands even more.

> It becomes easy to forget that the point of your life is not to enable your business. It's the other way around: the point of your business is to enable your life.

Good growth is about maintaining a steady pace and staying close to the people who matter. It means remembering your purpose and values, and building a network around that.

The alternative is a growth hangover. When ego demands you keep pedalling faster and faster, and your boundaries start to dissolve. Details get missed. Shortcuts get taken. The adrenalin keeps you going. Until it's too late, and excitement turns into resentment and then into regret.

How do you know which path to take?

When I was 14, my dad sat me down for some career advice. Knowing my knowledge of potential career paths was restricted to my known small world, he simply asked me to close my eyes. He wanted me to picture myself at the ripe old age of 25. What was I doing? Where was I? Who was I with? What did it feel like?

I described it to him as 'travelling around the world shopping with someone else's money'. By my mid-20s I was a retail buyer based in London, doing exactly that.

The idea to write this book began when I used the same approach and imagined what my next move – my encore career, perhaps – might look like.

So now it's your turn. Close your eyes.

Wait – read the next bit first. Then close your eyes.

Picture yourself in your work environment in a few years' time.

What are you doing? Who are you with? What sort of work are you doing – are you in front of a screen or leading a team? Where are you – in your spare room, in a co-working space, or somewhere you've never been? What does it feel like?

Make a note of any words that come to mind as you picture this. Does it feel scary? Exciting? Overwhelming? Rewarding? Maybe you've pictured some specific people you want around you – clients or colleagues. Jot down their names.

If working collaboratively was part of your picture, think about how you might assemble that team around you. Do you want to be the boss or form a more democratic cooperative?

If you saw yourself more as a soloist, surrounded by a variety of projects and income streams, start getting serious about that product strategy that's been playing in your subconscious for a while.

And if you saw yourself working from Europe in summer or Bali in winter, go for it. Stick to your freelance or fractional gigs, and maintain your boundaries.

Stepping out of your comfort zone

I was surrounded by children aged eight to fourteen, two of which were mine. We were about to attempt sailing in a large saltwater lake in precarious-looking dinghies. 'What's better, to stay in your comfort zone or push ourselves to try something that scares us?' asked the instructor.

'Stay in my comfort zone,' I said. 'Try something that scares us,' said every small child.

I realised then that my safety-first mindset was holding me back.

Around that time, I'd also realised my definition of what success meant to me was changing. When I first started my business, it was having control over my hours so I could have some time with my kids when they were still little.

Then they were at primary school, and my husband Jason and I wanted us to be able to travel as a family and give them a great education. We were happy to stay in a smaller house if we could do those two things. But we'd both also need to be able to draw more income from our two businesses and make sure that income was relatively stable.

That choice shaped my business strategy for the next few years. And, thanks to the camp sailing instructor, I was willing to step forward into growth and away from my comfort zone.

As my boys grew older and more independent, my definition of success changed again. I could picture having a place up the coast. I wasn't sure where exactly, but I could imagine it in vivid detail – a quiet place where I could write. A lifestyle where we could split our time between a home in the city and a home near the beach.

My husband was very much on board with this idea. But at the time, our bank balance was constantly drained by our mortgage and those other priorities we'd agreed on. It was definitely a 10-year-plus goal.

Several years later, after cancelling our winter school holiday plans thanks to COVID restrictions, we drove north and booked an Airbnb in a quiet coastal community some friends had suggested. As soon as I looked out across the headland at sunset, surrounded by ocean and national park, I looked at Jason and said, 'This is the place.'

A year later, we bought a house there. And, with the support of my team, Writers put a 'work from holiday house' policy in place. I'd like to think I do my most focused work up there – including writing this book.

This is what I mean by making the business work for you, not the other way around. It's also what success feels like to me today.

It's not a number on the profit and loss statement, but time. Time in a place that brings me peace and joy, working on something meaningful.

Start your engine

If you've already taken a leap of faith to work as a freelancer or consultant, that's an act of courage. You didn't let that idea wither and die. You took action. You did one thing. And then the next.

That's all you need to do now. You've just described what your ideal future looks like. Now's the fun part: what's one thing you can do tomorrow to get you there?

Your answer depends on where you are today. Here are a few ideas to help you prioritise the most important next step:

- Commit to your **purpose**. Go back to chapter 4, work out your why, then stick it somewhere you can see it.
- Check in with your clients. Ask a handful of good clients why they choose to work with you. Turn some common threads into your **proposition**. Make a note of five ways you could bring that message to life in your website, social posts, newsletter or pitch decks.
- Tap into some talent. If you made a note of someone specific you want on this journey with you – as an employee, collective member, referral partner or contractor – take them out for a coffee. Start building the right **people** into your network.
- Get your expertise out of your head. If outsourcing is part of your plan, you need to get those **processes** down on paper. Start with one regular task – like sending your newsletter or

creating a project timeline. Write down every step it takes, or record yourself talking through your process. Could a template save time? Could it turn into a product?
- Take control of your **profit**. Calculate your breakeven model. Work out how much profit you need at the end of the year, and then work backwards from there.

Start with one of those things *tomorrow*. Then move onto the next.

You are here

This is a milestone in your journey, where you get to choose which turn you take. And whether you take the freeway or the backroad, it's okay.

Peter Fuller says it's important to keep your perspective at each step. Especially when the road you end up on is an unexpected detour.

'We won't always achieve our financial goals or our biggest dreams,' he says. 'We will certainly have setbacks and balance our successes with the odd failure. People we employ and have high hopes for will leave us. Others you wish would leave refuse to. Some clients fail to understand how brilliant we are. Others love us to death.'

I can't think of a better way to describe the experience of running a small business. And despite all the ups and downs, it is always better than working for someone else.

Here's to you. Wherever you are on this journey, and wherever you choose to go next, I hope you feel more in control of your route. And I'd love to know where you end up going beyond solo.

Gratitude

There are people who have helped me build my business. There are people who have helped me turn this book from an idea that kept jumping up and down, demanding my attention, into something I can hold in my hands. And there are people who have made me a better person.

If those three groups were circles in a Venn diagram, there would be plenty of people in the intersections.

Right at the centre is Jason. Thank you for always believing in me, for being my fiercest advocate and strongest ally – and for giving us the financial stability to make time for this project. We make a great team.

In the business circle (and all the intersections), thank you to Renee, Loralle, Georgi, Mary and all the friends who have been my sales team, talent-scouters and let's-go-have-fun life coaches. Also my dad, who taught me everything I know about selling (one positive relationship at a time) and patiently coached me to find my confidence when I was too shy to put my hand up in my year 3 classroom.

A huge thanks to my team, past and present, for teaching me how to let go and for shaping our culture so magnificently. Thanks also to the founders of Writers Ltd in the UK for taking a chance on an Aussie would-be copywriter.

And to every client who trusted me with their words. I have learned so much from you all.

Then there is the circle of people who have helped me with this book. This book never would have made it into your hands without the calm midwifery of Anna, who pushed me to make this the best book I could create and reminded me to finish it. Thank you Rachel and Lynne for running the Content Byte Summit that led me to Anna. Also to my Content Summit 'alumni' mastermind group, who have also cheered me on, cheered me up and been a fantastic focus group. And of course, thanks to all the legendary business owners and freelancers who shared their stories with me with so much honesty and generosity. This is your book too.

Finally, to Sam and Dylan, who – more than anyone else in my life – have made me a better person. Being your mum has been the best part of the journey.

I would also like to share my sincere gratitude to you, the reader. Thank you for reading this far. I hope this book inspires a few ideas that will take you even further.

Acknowledgements

I am incredibly grateful to these business owners who shared their journey with me, with endless honesty and generosity. You are all legends.

- Amy Ragland
- Brooke Hill
- Carolyn Loton
- Carolyn Tate
- Ed Gandia
- Georgi Roberts
- Janine Pares
- Jessica White
- Jo Marshall
- Jordanne Collins
- Leif Kendall
- Lindy Alexander
- Matt Turner
- Oyelola Oyetunji
- Pete Cohen
- Peter Fuller
- Rachel Smith
- Sandra Muller
- Sarah Spence
- Simon Bedard
- Steph Sta Maria
- Sue-Ella McDowall
- Tyler Hakes

I've collated a Beyond Solo toolkit of practical checklists, cheat sheets and frameworks. Including the very nerdy Breakeven Model Spreadsheet. You'll find them all at:

beyondsolo.co

www.ingramcontent.com/pod-product-compliance
Lightning Source LLC
LaVergne TN
LVHW041625060526
838200LV00040B/1441